Fresh Food
IN A JAR

Fresh Food
IN A JAR

PICKLING, FREEZING, DRYING & CANNING

MADE EASY

KIMBERLEY WILLIS

Globe
Pequot

GUILFORD, CONNECTICUT

Globe Pequot

An imprint of Rowman & Littlefield

Distributed by NATIONAL BOOK NETWORK

Copyright © 2016 by Rowman & Littlefield

British Library Cataloguing in Publication Information Available

Library of Congress Cataloging-in-Publication Data Available

ISBN 978-1-4930-2453-7 (paperback)
ISBN 978-1-4930-2454-4 (e-book)

∞™ The paper used in this publication meets the minimum requirements of American National Standard for Information Sciences—Permanence of Paper for Printed Library Materials, ANSI/NISO Z39.48-1992.

To my husband, Steve: Thanks for doing the housework again while I write!

ACKNOWLEDGMENTS

I'd like to thank my hardworking agent, Barb Doyen; friendly, helpful editors, Lara Asher and Katie Sharp; and artistic photographer, Viktor Budnik, for their help in making this book a success.

PHOTOGRAPHER ACKNOWLEDGMENTS

I would like to say thanks to everyone at Globe Pequot and to Kim Willis. It is a real pleasure to be on a team with great people. Thank you also goes to my crew of gifted and talented people: Claire Stancer—a wonderful and great food stylist—created beautiful food to shoot; Celeste kept us on schedule and did all the shopping for the book; and Kimmi, a truly great assistant.

Cheers,
Viktor Budnik

CONTENTS

INTRODUCTION

Some of you may have helped someone else can or preserve food when you were young, but many of you are at least a generation away from knowing anyone who actually preserved some of his or her own food. You may be interested in knowing how to preserve food but don't know how to start. This book was written to give you a quick and easy introduction to the basics of preserving your own food.

Our ancestors preserved food because it was the only way to ensure that their family had a good variety of food—and enough food—over the winter months. People grew their own produce or bought it locally and spent a great deal of the summer preserving it for winter. It was survival.

Then freezers, refrigerated trucks, and chilled grocery cases were introduced, which made finding fresh food in the grocery store easier. Women increasingly worked outside the home, and there was less time to preserve food at home. Grocery food was cheap and available, and most people stopped preserving food at home.

In the 1970s many people became interested in survival and back-to-the-land movements, and canning and other methods of home food preservation enjoyed a brief spike in popularity. That soon ebbed as people found that living off the land was harder than they planned, and those who did find it comfortable began to age and look for easier "harvests."

Forty years later canning and other methods of home food preservation are again drawing interest. This time it's not because we can't get cheap food of almost any kind in any season, but because we want to control the quality and safety of the food we eat. We actually want *better*, not cheaper, food. We want to eat locally and seasonally, which is ecologically sound, but not feel deprived when some foods are out of season. We also want to be able to preserve that healthy, local food so we don't have to resort to chemical-laden food, picked green, handled by who knows who, and shipped thousands of miles when the season is over.

When you preserve food at home, you control the quality of the food, the cleanliness of its preparation, and its seasonings. Because you and those you love are going to eat that food, you will do everything you can to make sure the food is safe to eat.

Some of you are also frugal and feel that preserving food is a good way to save money. After your initial investment in a canner or freezer and other supplies, you may actually save money, especially if you have an abundance of homegrown food. But saving money shouldn't be your only motivation.

If prepared properly, home-preserved food is as safe, if not safer, than purchased food. It has more vitamins, fewer chemicals, and a smaller chance of causing food-borne illnesses than commercially prepared food. And most important—it tastes better! You can customize home-preserved food to your taste preferences.

Preserving food at home is easier than it used to be, thanks to modern food prep machinery, such as food processors, and the fact that modern homes often have air-conditioning to offset hot kitchens. But food preservation still requires time and close attention to details.

Start small; don't start with six bushels of produce to can on your first attempt. Read the recipe carefully, paying attention to everything you'll need and the amount of time it takes to complete that recipe. In this book ingredients are listed in the order they are used. Allow yourself plenty of time. It's a rush-rush world, but preserving your own food is not a project to rush through or do haphazardly.

Food-preservation recipes, especially canning recipes, cannot be experimented with safely, unlike other types of cooking. If the recipe doesn't give you permission to adjust ingredients, then don't do so. Measure carefully and accurately. Some ingredients, or the amount of an ingredient in ratio to other ingredients, affect the safety of the stored food. Always follow the type of processing recommended, and the amount of time it requires, exactly. Throughout the book, each canning recipe includes a separate processing chart for easy reference.

Use modern recipes, especially for canning. Modern recipes are generally based on research done by the USDA and universities across the country to provide the safest and most nutritious foods. The recipes in this book are carefully based on USDA procedures and recommendations.

If you want safe, nutritious, and flavorful food, you have to start with it. Don't use old, spoiled, overripe, diseased, or damaged produce or meat for preserving. Use any damaged or overripe food immediately and preserve your best food. Canning, drying, or freezing spoiled food won't make it safe to eat.

Even if you start with the best quality, safest food, you can contaminate it during preparation. Keep your hands clean and scrub your sink and countertops before beginning to prepare food. Wash jars and containers before filling with food, and sterilize jars if the recipe calls for it.

During preparation, cover any food waiting to be used to prevent insect contamination. Always scrub cutting boards and utensils used on meat with hot water and soap, then rinse well before using them on produce or other food.

E. coli, salmonella, and botulism are responsible for most cases of food poisoning in home-preserved foods. All three are preventable if you follow all proper cleaning, processing, and recipe instructions. Botulism is by far the most deadly and almost always occurs in low-acid foods such as vegetables and meat that are canned. Be particularly careful canning these foods.

You are responsible for "recalls" on food you preserve at home. If you find or suspect that food wasn't processed correctly or it looks odd colored, smells bad, or is otherwise suspicious, you must make the decision on what to do.

Always err on the side of safety. Don't taste suspected foods, and discard them where pets and children can't find them. Consult with an expert canner or call a hotline or consult with a food educator at your local Cooperative Extension office if you want, but ultimately it's your call.

To find an Extension office, you can go to: www.csrees.usda.gov/Extension/USA-text.html. Extension offices are educational outreach sites for universities or colleges in your state in partnership with the USDA.

Enough of the scary things. Once you get the hang of it, you'll enjoy preserving food or at least enjoy eating it and serving it proudly to family and friends. Millions of people around the world preserve some or all of their food—you can do it, too. If you are growing some of that food, it's even better.

Let's take a look at one common food, the tomato, to see the impact that growing and using local food has on the environment and the economy. While commercially canned tomatoes are generally grown near where they are processed, fossil fuel is still used to get those cans to the warehouse and then to stores thousands of miles away. And labels and boxes have to be made for labeling and transporting the cans.

Lots of pesticides are used on most commercial tomato crops. Chemicals are also used to make a liner for the cans, some of which are now suspected

of leaching into the food and causing problems. The production of all those chemicals and the metal cans create a lot of industrial waste as they are produced.

And if those tomatoes are canned in a country with low food-safety standards, who knows what goes into those cans? What's more, canned tomatoes often have salt and sometimes other spices added to them. You can make your home-canned tomatoes salt free, or you can season them just the way you like them.

Now if you can wean yourself off those expensive, hard, tasteless, pesticide-coated "fresh" tomatoes flown in from South America in the middle of winter so you can have a salad, you'll be a very "green" person. Just use your home-canned diced tomatoes on the salad, and instead enjoy juicy, sun-ripened, real tomato flavor.

So get reading. Use this book to fill your cupboards with gleaming jars of home-canned foods and your freezer full of neat packages of perfectly frozen foods. Go green and enjoy the best food ever.

TYPES OF CANNERS
THERE ARE TWO TYPES OF CANNERS: WATER BATH AND PRESSURE

The two basic types of canners used in this book are the water-bath canner, which essentially boils jars of food, and the pressure canner, which uses pressure to get food to cook at a temperature higher than boiling. Pressure canners are divided into two main types, those that use a dial to adjust the pressure and those that use weights.

Canners can be made of aluminum, enameled steel, or stainless steel. The most practical size canner for home canning is one that holds 7 quarts or 8 to 9 pint jars. All canners should come with a rack for jars. Some have a rack that allows two layers of pint jars.

Used canners can be a good deal if all the parts and instructions are still intact. Since pressure canners

CHOOSING A CANNER

If you will only be canning fruits, tomatoes with added acid, pickles, jams, and jellies, you could just buy a water-bath canner.

If you intend to can vegetables other than tomatoes, or meats and soups, you will need a pressure canner.

A pressure canner can be used as a water-bath canner, but the opposite doesn't work. Water-bath canning usually takes less time.

Pressure canners with dial gauges need the gauge checked yearly. See Chapter 20 for information.

PRESSURE CANNERS

Pressure canners work by building up pressure inside the canner so food cooks at a temperature hotter than boiling.

Temperatures above boiling are needed to kill harmful bacteria and fungi in low-acid foods.

With dial pressure canners, you read the pressure on the dial and adjust the heat to maintain the pressure needed.

With weighted pressure canners, you adjust weights on a vent to change the pressure. Follow all canner instructions carefully.

have several different methods of locking the lids and adjusting the pressure, having the instruction manual is critical.

If a pressure canner is old or has seen a lot of use, the rubber gasket on the lid may need to be replaced. The dial on a pressure canner that uses one needs to be checked each year. See Chapter 20 for resources for this.

The canner should not be more than 4 inches larger in diameter than your largest burner. Canners that will be used on electric ranges need to have flat bottoms.

Important

Steam canners are fairly new. They have a shallow pan to which you add a few cups of water and then a high domed lid that fits over the canning jars. Steam heats the jars. Some recent research suggests they can be used safely for the same foods as a water-bath canner. However the processing charts in this book should not be used with steam canners.

WATER-BATH CANNERS

Water-bath canners heat jars of food in boiling water. They have a rack to hold jars off the canner floor.

Water-bath canning is safe for high-acid foods only. Always follow the recipe directions for the type of canner to use.

Water must cover the jars in the canner by at least 2 inches for safe canning.

At higher altitudes water boils at a lower temperature, so adjust the amount of time for processing food by your altitude.

HOW THE CANNER WORKS

Canners work from the heat of the burners on your stove. Gas or electric burners are fine.

Never use the oven, a microwave oven, or Crock-Pot to can.

You adjust the heat on your stove to keep the water boiling or the correct pressure going in your canner.

If the water stops boiling in water-bath canners or the pressure drops in pressure canners, you must start counting processing time all over once the boiling or correct pressure is resumed.

JARS & LIDS

Most large retail stores now carry canning jars and lids, at least in the summer months. There are numerous sources online and through mail order for jars and lids if you can't find them locally. (See Chapter 20 for sources to buy jars.) Buying jars can be considered an investment, because if you take good care of them you can reuse them for many years.

Buy jars that are standard American measures, such as quart, pint, and half-pint for ease in following recipes and processing times. Make sure they have standard openings so that you don't have to hunt down special lids every time you use them.

Buy jars that are labeled for canning and not storage. Some jars are also freezer safe now. Plain jars

SIZES AND TYPES OF JARS

Common jar sizes are quart, pint, and half-pint. These may have regular mouths or wide mouths.

Widemouthed jars allow you to place larger pieces of food into the jars, such as large pickles. They are processed like the same size jar with a regular mouth.

Jars come with rounded or square sides. There is no difference in processing time between the two.

For best results use the jar size called for in a recipe. It isn't safe to guess at processing time.

TYPES OF LIDS

Modern lids are actually two pieces: the "lid" and the screw band. The lid has a ring of sealant that makes an airtight seal on the jar rim.

The seal is made when canned food cools and contracts, creating a vacuum and pulling the lid down in the center.

Screw bands are removed after the jar has cooled and can be reused. Lids cannot be reused.

Plastic storage caps can protect jar lids from rusting or being knocked loose.

will cost you less, but fancy embossed jars may be your choice if you like to give away jars of canned food. Embossed jars are as safe as plain jars to use.

You can buy used jars if they are clean and you examine them carefully for chips and cracks. Even unused lids may not seal well after a few years of storage, so buy new lids. Screw rims are reusable, but the inner lid is not.

Colored Jars

The color of a jar doesn't affect food safety. Most modern jars are clear, but occasionally blue or green jars still show up. People used to think that the color of the jar kept the food inside from discoloring in storage and kept the vitamin content from being lost. This won't happen if you store jars correctly. You can use any color jar if it is made for canning.

JARS AND LIDS NOT TO USE

Glass lids with wire bails or rubber stoppers are not safe to use for canning.

Old porcelain-lined metal caps that are used with rubber rings are no longer considered safe for canning.

Jars recycled from commercially canned foods should not be used for home canning. They are not manufactured to withstand home-canning methods. The rims may not fit home-canning lids.

Jars with cracks or noticeable scratches or that have chipped rims are not safe to use.

STERILIZING JARS

Jars should be washed in hot, soapy water before use. They should be sterilized if they will be processed for less than 10 minutes in a water-bath canner.

To sterilize, place jars in a large pot with 2 inches of water over the top of the jars.

Bring the water to a boil and boil 15 minutes. Keep jars hot until filled.

A dishwasher with a sterilize setting can be used to sterilize jars. Keep them hot until filled.

SPECIALIZED EQUIPMENT

THESE ITEMS ARE HIGHLY RECOMMENDED TO MAKE CANNING EASIER AND SAFER

When you first begin canning, you may want to keep your equipment purchases small. There are certain things that are helpful, however, that will make your canning experience much more pleasant. These items will keep you from getting hurt in the process of canning and also aid with food safety.

You can safely look for bargains at garage sales and flea markets. Older but serviceable equipment is often for sale. Some of the older gadgets may be hard to find today, but the hardest part for many people is knowing how to use those gadgets! You may want to ask older relatives and friends if they have canning equipment they no longer use.

JAR AND LID LIFTERS

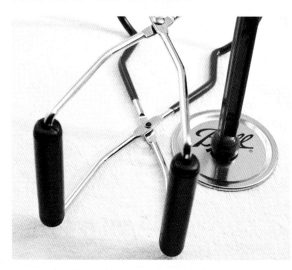

Canner racks may be too heavy for many people to safely lift when they are filled with jars.

Jar lifters allow you to move one jar at a time and keep your fingers away from boiling water.

The grip part of the jar lifter is placed under the screw band. Jars are lifted or lowered while in an upright position, never tilted.

Lid lifters have a magnet so that slippery lids can be easily grasped and lifted from hot water.

JAR FUNNELS AND BUBBLE STICKS

Unlike cone-shaped funnels, jar funnels fit securely on jars so you don't have to hold them in place.

Pint and quart jars generally have the same size mouth openings, and the same funnels can be used on both. Widemouthed funnels will be needed if you use wide-mouth jars.

Bubble sticks remove trapped air from jars before processing so less shrinkage occurs.

Bubble sticks are often combined with lid lifters. Never use metal objects in the jars.

PROPER WAY TO OPEN JARS

LABELS ARE ESSENTIAL

Jars should be opened carefully so you don't damage them and can reuse them.

A jar wrench is used to remove screw bands that are on too tightly or have rusted onto jars. It is not used to tighten screw bands.

A lid opener breaks the lid seal without damaging the jar rim.

Lid openers are old-fashioned bottle openers with squared ends, not a punch end. Plastic or rubber-coated metal is best to avoid scratching the rim.

Although you can see what's inside, canned food should be labeled.

The food name and the date it was canned are the most important things to put on each jar. You may want to note seasonings, too.

Dating jars makes it easy to rotate food. Properly canned food may be good for several years but is better if consumed within 12 months.

If you plan to reuse jars, place stick-on labels on lids, not jar sides, or write on lids.

FOOD-PREP EQUIPMENT
SOME ITEMS MAKE PREPARING FOOD FOR CANNING EASIER

Some food-processing equipment for canning is rather specialized, but other things may already be in your kitchen. If you believe that you will be canning on a large scale, food-processing equipment will make the job much easier.

Modern electric equipment is great, but even some hand-cranked food-processing equipment can be a big help. Buy what you can afford and what seems practical for the job at hand. Equipment that has multiple applications other than canning makes a larger purchase more justified.

Once again look for used equipment to save money, and ask relatives and friends if they have equipment they can give or loan to you. You may

FOOD SCALES

Many older canning recipes list weights of foods instead of standard amounts. To use them safely, you must carefully weigh ingredients.

Weighing your food surplus may give you a quick answer as to whether you have enough of an item to make a certain recipe.

New digital scales make reading the scale easy but are slightly more expensive.

Food scales have many uses in the kitchen. A good food scale has the capability of weighing both ounces and pounds.

FOOD PROCESSORS FOR PREP

If you do small amounts of canning, a small inexpensive food processor will probably handle many prep steps for you.

If you plan to do large-scale canning, a processor that handles large quantities and has a variety of blades and attachments can be a major help.

Most food processors do not have a straining feature, something that separates seeds and skin.

Some prep work cannot be handled by food processors, such as peeling and coring.

want to borrow a piece of equipment to use before you buy one, to see if the time and effort it saved you is worth the cost.

Larger is not necessarily better; even large canning jobs may require only minimum amounts of food processing—for example, chopping one or two onions. Small choppers may work just as well.

Small handheld submersion blenders allow you to smooth some food right in the pot while it cooks and can save you time. However, they are impractical for large, deep pots of food.

FOOD STRAINERS ARE HANDY

Food strainers, sometimes called food mills, are essential if you intend to make seedless jams or certain juices and sauces.

A hand-cranked food mill can work for small canning jobs. Even regular kitchen strainers and colanders can be used for straining small amounts of food.

Large electric food mills may also peel or slice foods and are great for large jobs.

Many foods need to be blanched or softened before being put into the strainer.

USING A JELLY BAG

Jelly bags are used to make clear juices and jellies. The stand holds the bag over a bowl or pot.

A jelly bag can be improvised by lining a colander or strainer with two layers of cheesecloth.

Crushed food is put into a jelly bag and the juices are slowly allowed to seep through the material.

Moisten bags before food is put in them. Never squeeze or press the food; let juices drip out into the bowl.

OTHER FOOD-PREP TOOLS
MANY OF THESE ITEMS ARE ALREADY IN YOUR KITCHEN

One of the top food-processing tools in the kitchen is your stove, of course. Both types of canners recommended in this book need to sit on a stove top to heat. Stoves with one or two extra-large burners are especially helpful when it comes to heating canners and large stock pots.

Before air-conditioning became common, people who did a lot of summer canning often had a stove outside or in the basement. Canning can be hot, steamy work. If you don't have air-conditioning, a good fan is an essential piece of equipment.

Since cooling jars of canned food can take up a lot of counter space for many hours, you may want an extra table that is sturdy and heatproof. Your counters and tabletops will need clean towels or wire racks on them to hold hot jars. This protects jars from

PEELING AND SLICING TOOLS

Processing food for canning requires some good paring and slicing knives. Keep them sharp.

Specialty prep tools, like the apple corer and slicer, and apple peelers, are handy if you process lots of apples.

There are special peelers for peaches and other soft fruit and tools that pit cherries.

Mandoline slicers keep fingers safe and allow you to make decorative slices. Corn cutters remove kernels from the cobs quickly and safely.

CANNING REQUIRES EXACT MEASUREMENTS

Several sets of measuring spoons and cups should be available for canning.

Glass and metal measuring cups are probably safer around heat than plastic measuring cups. Find utensils with easy-to-read markings.

Don't substitute things like teacups and tableware for measuring spoons and cups. Canning measurements need to be exact in many cases.

A set of plastic tubs with lids is handy to store measured ingredients until they are used.

contact with cold surfaces, which can crack them, and allows them to cool faster.

And of course most kitchens have pots and pans, slicing and dicing tools, peelers, graters, ladles, spoons, and even things like melon ballers and garlic presses, which are all useful when processing food for canning. Before beginning, check your kitchen for these items and have them ready to use.

Don't Forget an Apron

Don't forget an apron. An apron keeps food from splashing on your clothes and often has a handy pocket to hold essential items—and you always have something to wipe your hands on. There are aprons designed for men or women. If you do a lot of canning, you may want to invest in heavy-duty, water-resistant aprons. If you have lots of small helpers, buy a box of plastic disposable food-service aprons.

COLANDERS AND STRAINERS

Having several sizes of colanders and strainers is very helpful when canning. Colanders generally have larger holes than strainers.

For canning, stainless steel or aluminum colanders and strainers are preferred over plastic.

Your colanders and strainers should be large enough to rest on the rims of your pots so you don't have to hold them. Some colanders have stands.

Large colanders that are squared and fit over a sink are excellent for washing produce.

POTS AND PANS

In addition to the canner, you need saucepans or stockpots for precooking, blanching, and processing food.

Stockpots generally have straight sides, two handles, and a lid. Saucepans usually have one longer handle.

At least one stockpot should be large enough to hold a complete load of jars with 1 to 2 inches of water over the top to sterilize jars or keep them hot.

The best material for saucepans and stockpots is stainless steel or aluminum.

PRESERVATIVES & SPICES
SPICES AND PRESERVATIVES RUN FROM BASIC TO EXOTIC

In some canning recipes certain ingredients, such as vinegar, are essential as preservatives, and in other recipes they provide flavoring. Sugar, salt, and lemon juice can also be essential or just flavors. Unless you know for sure that an ingredient is just for flavoring, never omit it or change the quantity.

Salt is generally a preservative in pickling recipes, and amounts shouldn't be altered. In recipes where just a small amount of salt is used, it is usually a flavoring and can be omitted. Sugar is essential in most jam and jelly recipes to make the juices jell. In canning fruits, some fruits look better and have a better texture when canned in syrups made with sugar.

Canning your own food allows you to adjust spices to suit your taste or to remove spices that aggravate allergies. In general, spices are for flavoring and the

VINEGAR

SALT AND SUGAR

Vinegar for canning should always be 5 percent acidity, whether it's white or cider vinegar. Anything else may result in food spoilage.

Buy commercial vinegar for canning so the acidity is always known.

Cider vinegar does have a slightly different taste, but usually the type of vinegar only matters for looks; white vinegar makes a clear liquid.

Vinegar is usually part of the preservative for a canned product, and the amount in a recipe should not be changed.

Salt used in canning should be labeled for canning or pickling. Kosher salt can also be used. This salt does not have iodine or other additives.

Beet or cane sugar is fine for canning. Do not use any sugar with additives. Brown sugar is used for flavor in some recipes.

Honey or corn syrup can sometimes be substituted in recipes for sugar, but they add their own flavors.

Don't use artificial sweeteners or salt substitutes unless the recipe calls for it.

amounts can be altered or omitted entirely. However, if you take away the dill, your pickles won't taste like dill pickles. Removing other spices may also remove a unique flavor associated with that product.

Try a small batch with your substitutions or omissions before processing huge quantities, and taste it to see if it's what you expected.

Spices

Some canning spices are seldom used in other cooking. Buy small quantities that can be used in one season and keep them in dry, airtight containers. Spices lose flavor quickly after being opened. Seasoning packets that contain spice mixtures can be a good buy for small batches. Buying spices separately gives you more control over what and how much goes into your canned product.

PRESERVATIVES, THICKENERS, AND ACIDIFIERS

Lemon juice can be used like vinegar to acidify foods for safe canning. It's also used to preserve color in fruits.

Citric and ascorbic acid can be found with canning supplies and are used to acidify food or preserve fruit color.

Pectin causes fruit juices to jell. Some pectins need extra sugar to work; others work without it.

Cornstarch and other thickeners should not be used in canned foods. To thicken fillings for canning, use Clear Jel only.

FLAVORING

Whole spices can be tied in cheesecloth or put in a tea ball and used to flavor foods that are precooked.

Some whole spices are used in jars for flavor and appearance, such as dill flowers.

Substituting powdered spices for whole may produce a cloudy appearance or sediment on the bottom of the jar.

Be careful when using spices not called for in recipes. Some spices become bitter or develop off flavors during the canning process.

CANNING SAFELY

ALL CANNING REQUIRES LEARNING SOME FOOD SAFETY RULES

Botulism and other types of food poisoning can occur in both home-canned and commercially canned food. Food poisoning can be deadly. When you decide to preserve food for you and your family, you are the one responsible for seeing that it is preserved safely.

Any food you can should be of top quality, not a reject you don't want at your table. Overripe, damaged, diseased, or moldy produce or meat that hasn't been stored properly is more likely to spoil in canning than quality food.

Cleanliness is always important. Wash produce thoroughly before processing it. Wash jars, rims, lids, and canners in hot, soapy water and rinse well before use.

Follow canning recipes exactly when it comes to jar

Knowing How to Process Foods

A water-bath canner is used to can acidic foods such as fruits and for tomatoes that have additional acid added.

A pressure canner is needed to can vegetables and meat.

Jams, jellies, and pickles are usually canned in a water-bath canner, but follow recipe directions.

Mixtures of vegetables and fruits, such as sauces and salsas, can be canned with water-bath canners or pressure canners, depending on how acidic the mix is. Follow the recipe directions exactly.

USE PRECISE MEASUREMENTS

Changing the amount or proportion of ingredients in a recipe can make the processing time unsafe, especially in fruit and vegetable mixtures canned in a water-bath canner.

Never alter the amount given for vinegar, lemon juice, or citric acid which is used to acidify recipes.

Don't alter the amount of fluids added to recipes, unless the recipe suggests it for certain circumstances.

Use the jar size called for in the recipe. Altering the size can make the processing time unsafe.

sizes and processing times. And process food in the correct type of canner.

If you discover that your pressure canner isn't working correctly, or that you made a mistake in following the recipe or timing, and the food has been canned for more than 24 hours, you probably need to discard that food. At the very least, consult with a canning expert at your Cooperative Extension office or other reliable source (see Chapter 20).

If you discover a mistake before 24 hours has passed, you can reprocess the food or freeze it.

Important

Dispose of spoiled canned food where children and pets can't find it. Foods suspected of being contaminated with botulism are hazardous waste and need to be treated before disposal. Wearing gloves (botulism can be absorbed through skin), carefully place unopened jars in a large pot, cover with water, and boil for 30 minutes. Wash gloves with hot water and soap before removing them. Discard jars with contents.

CLEAN, HOT JARS AND LIDS

Wash all jars, lids, and rims with hot, soapy water and rinse well before using.

Sterilize jars that will be processed in a boiling water canner for less than 10 minutes. Jars going into a pressure canner do not need to be sterilized.

Keep jars and lids waiting to be filled submerged in clean hot water.

Fill jars while hot and have water simmering in the canner to place them in as you fill them.

FOOD POISONING

Any canned food that looks or smells bad should be discarded. Do not taste it.

If a jar appears to be unsealed, don't taste the food inside.

Signs of spoiled food include leaking jars, mold, dried food on top of contents, discoloration, bulging lids, spurting gas or liquid when opened, or lids that lift too easily. Discard those jars.

Botulism can occur in sealed jars if the food was processed incorrectly. It's most likely to occur in low-acid foods.

PREPARING FOOD

WASHING, PEELING, CORING, AND CUTTING ARE ALL PART OF FOOD PREPARATION

Often the most tedious and time-consuming part of canning is the food preparation. But preparing food correctly ensures that it will taste good and process correctly.

Some food preparations seem complex, but after you have processed a bushel or two you will get the hang of it and become faster at the process.

While children may not be able to safely help with the actual canning process, they can often help you prepare the food. They can take pride in helping the family store healthy food and may be more inclined to eat it. Many of us who are interested in canning today remember helping someone can when we were younger.

WASHING AND PEELING

Scrub root vegetables with a brush under running water to remove all dirt. Any purchased produce that was waxed needs to be washed with soap to remove the wax.

Soak cabbage and spinach in 1 tablespoon salt to a gallon of water to remove insects.

Don't wash berries, grapes, and peaches until just before you use them.

Some fruits and vegetables don't require peeling. Check the recipe first.

SLICING AND DICING

You are less likely to be cut with a sharp knife because you use less pressure to cut.

Check the recipe. Food may be measured before cutting or by cups of cut, peeled produce.

The thickness and size of food pieces can make a difference in processing time.

For food that discolors as it sits, slice directly into a color-preservative solution of 1 cup lemon juice or 3 grams ascorbic acid to 1 gallon water.

Sometimes the way you prepare the raw ingredients can make them visually appealing as well as tasty. Instead of plain round carrot slices, make them waffle or wavy slices. Children often find small pieces more appealing than larger ones.

Remember to consult the recipe for how thick some foods should be sliced. The thickness of the food may determine the processing time. Don't puree or mash foods unless the recipe calls for it, because the density of the product will change the processing time.

BLANCHING

Blanching is dipping food in simmering water then plunging it into cold water. Putting food in a colander makes it easier.

Blanching makes peeling easier on some foods and is used on other foods to inactivate enzymes that cause spoilage or off flavors.

For peeling, dip food in simmering water for about 1 minute. For inactivating enzymes, follow the recipe for the produce you're using.

Don't leave food in simmering water too long. It can destroy texture and flavor.

PRECOOKING FOOD

Many recipes call for precooking the ingredients before they are canned. This can be a few minutes or hours.

Precooking is used to soften foods so they can be blended, to flavor them with spices, to increase food safety, or to shorten processing time.

Follow recipe directions and don't under- or overcook food. This can alter the flavor or texture or cause food to spoil.

Jars are usually filled with the hot food immediately after precooking.

METHODS OF CANNING

HOT PACK AND COLD PACK ARE THE TWO METHODS OF PROCESSING; JAMS, JELLIES, AND PICKLES ARE ALSO CANNED

In earlier days food was often cooked in a large pot and poured into jars, and the jars were left on the table to hopefully cool, contract, and seal. This method of canning, called the open-kettle method, is no longer recommended. We modify this method today by precooking the food, pouring it into hot, clean jars, and then processing it in a water-bath canner or pressure canner. This is called a hot pack.

If prepared raw food is packed into jars, and then a hot fluid is poured in around them before processing, it is called the raw pack or cold pack method,

HOT PACK

Many recipes call for the food to be precooked or at least heated to boiling and then poured into jars.

Hot-packed jars have less shrinkage of food during processing and are less likely to have excess headspace in the jars after processing.

Use a funnel to pour hot food into the jar to avoid wasting food.

Try to get equal amounts of solid food and cooking liquid in each jar. All food should be surrounded and covered by fluid.

COLD OR RAW PACK

A few recipes call for raw food to be arranged in jars, and then a hot fluid is poured over them before processing.

Cold-packed foods often experience shrinkage during processing. Most foods should be packed tightly in jars because of this.

Beans, peas, corn, and potatoes should not be packed tightly into jars for cold packing. They expand during processing.

Fluid should completely cover and surround the food in each jar. Remove the bubbles before processing.

although it really isn't cold. These foods are also processed in a canner.

Pickles can be made by the hot pack or cold pack method or by allowing them to ferment in crocks. To can fermented food for long-term storage, it is processed in a canner, usually a water-bath canner because it is very acidic.

Jams and jellies are hot packs because the food is cooked before the jars are filled. In earlier days wax was melted and poured on top of jelly and jam jars to form a seal. Today jams and jellies are processed in a canner or are stored in the freezer.

CANNING JAMS AND JELLIES

Jams, jellies, and preserves are always precooked, because heat is required to make the fruit juice gel.

Foam is often produced during the cooking process. This should be skimmed off before pouring food into jars.

Jars must be sterilized before jam or jelly is poured into them. Home-canned jam and jelly make better gel in half-pint or smaller jars.

Don't process jars more than 5 minutes, or they may soften and lose their gel.

CANNING PICKLES

Pickles are generally canned in a water-bath canner. They can be hot or raw packed.

Do not boil vinegar mixes longer than the recipe calls for, or you may weaken the acidity and affect the preservation of the pickles.

Follow the recipe for headspace and make sure you remove bubbles before processing.

You may want to use wide-mouth jars when canning whole cucumber pickles. Don't wedge the pickles in so tightly that they are hard to remove.

FILLING JARS

PROPERLY FILLING YOUR JARS WILL RESULT IN A GOOD SEAL AND THE BEST TASTING, SAFEST FOOD

Canning jars should always be warm or hot when they are filled. Until they are ready to be filled, they should be submerged in a pot of simmering water. Your lids and rims should also be kept in warm water, but read the directions on the lid package to see if any temperature recommendations are given.

A dishwasher with a warm cycle can also be used to keep your jars and lids hot and ready for you.

Get all your ingredients measured, mixed, precooked, or heated before removing the jars. Lift them with tongs or jar lifters, drain water, and set them on clean dishcloths or paper towels upside

PROPER FILLING OF JARS

It's very hard to pour food into jars from a hot pot, even with a funnel. Using a ladle gives you better control.

If you are raw packing food into the jars, make sure your hands are clean.

Fill jars so they have the recommended amount of headspace. Until you get a feel for that, measure the first jar and compare the others to it.

Adjust jars so they have equal amounts of solids and fluids if possible.

REMOVING AIR BUBBLES

When jars are filled, especially if raw packed, pieces of food may trap air bubbles on their surfaces and between them.

When the food is heated during processing, the air bubbles rise to the top of the jar and create a big air space.

After filling jars, slowly run a bubble stick through the food and between the jar sides and the food to release bubbles. Don't stir.

Add more food or fluid if the bubble removal creates space.

down on the counter. Invert each one just before you fill it. In some recipes, you add salt or spices to each jar before you fill it. Make sure to read all the recipe instructions so this doesn't come as a surprise to you after you have filled the jars.

Your canner should be on the stove pre-heating with some water in it. Filling the canner rack and then lowering it into the canner can be very hard, especially when it's full of quart jars. It's easier to lower individual jars into the canner.

WIPING THE RIM

Before placing the lid on the jar, wipe the rim with a moist paper towel.

This step is important because any food or liquid on the rim will prevent a good seal.

When moving jars into the canner, they must be kept upright so that food doesn't slosh and possibly get under the lid.

Even a bit of fat or salt grains can prevent a good seal, so make sure rims are wiped clean.

PUTTING ON THE LIDS

After the rim is clean, place the lid on the jar with the ring of sealant down.

Place a screw band on the jar and, holding the lid in place with your fingers, tighten the screw band.

Tighten the band firmly but don't over tighten. Air needs to escape during processing.

Keep the jar flat on the table while you put on the lid and band and don't move jars until the lid is secure. Keep jars upright when you move them.

PROCESSING JARS
THERE ARE TWO WAYS OF PROCESSING: WATER-BATH AND PRESSURE CANNING

Once you have your jars properly filled, they are ready to process. Your recipe will tell you what type of canner to use. That canner should be pre-heating on your stove before you begin filling the jars.

Water-bath canning takes the least amount of time but is not suitable for all types of food. Some foods canned in a pressure canner can take a very long time to process one batch.

If you have your timer in your pocket to keep track of time, you can leave the kitchen for short periods but don't go too far. Canning jars have been known to explode. Stay vigilant and keep the water boiling

Adjusting Processing Time by Altitude

Where you live affects canning safety. Water boils at a lower temperature the higher above sea level you are and the lower temperatures take longer to kill harmful bacteria.

Food must be processed longer at higher altitudes or under higher pressure.

In this book most recipes include a chart to help you to determine how to process food depending on your altitude.

To find your altitude, you can ask your Cooperative Extension office, county government, or go online and look up your address on any mapping program. See Chapter 20 for suggestions.

FILLING AND ADJUSTING CANNERS

Fill water-bath canners half-full of water and begin heating as you fill the jars.

After the jars are in the canner, remove or add water to get the level to the proper 2 inches above the jars.

For pressure canners, read your instruction manual for how much water to put in to preheat and process.

If the pressure canner has a rubber gasket on the lid, make sure it's clean before use.

or the pressure at the right setting, or you will have to start timing all over.

For water-bath canners it's a good idea to have some boiling water in another pot to add to the canner if the water level drops. Cooler water will cause the canner to stop boiling and you'll need to start timing all over.

Expect your first canning adventure to take longer than planned. As you gain experience and get a feel for how to manage your time, you'll be able to process many batches in the same day if you need to.

Canning Parties

In the good old days, women often got together and had canning parties at each other's houses. If you enjoy company in the kitchen, the big job will seem like fun with many hands helping and much gossiping going on. Add some good music and a little wine (or beer), and canning won't seem so hard at all. And in today's world you don't need to restrict your helpers to women; you can invite the guys, too.

WHEN TO START TIMING

For water-bath canners, start timing as soon as the water begins to boil after the jars have been put in the canner.

Pressure canners must vent before you actually begin timing the canning process.

After pressure canners have vented, close the vent and wait for the dial to reach the right pressure or for the weights to begin rocking or jiggling to begin timing.

Timing is critical to food safety, so set a timer or pay close attention to a clock.

VENTING STEAM ON PRESSURE CANNERS

Follow your canner directions for the amount of water to add to a pressure canner.

Put the lid on and bring the water to a boil with the vent open on high heat. Steam should come out of the vent.

Let steam vent for 10 minutes. Then close the vent or add weights and lower the heat to a medium setting.

The heat is lowered because you may need to raise it after the pressure is reached to keep the correct pressure.

REMOVE, COOL & STORE

PROPER COOLING IS PART OF THE PROCESSING, AND STORING FOOD CORRECTLY KEEPS IT SAFE

Before you begin your canning adventure, make sure you have a safe spot where the jars can sit and cool for up to 24 hours. Children and other curious people should not handle the jars during the cooling process.

When the jars are cool and you have checked the seals and labeled them, it's time to move them to storage. A plastic storage cap is highly recommended. This is put on over the lid, after the screw band is removed. It keeps the lid clean and rust free in storage and gives you something to cover an opened jar with if it isn't used completely. (Refrigerate opened jars.)

COOL DOWN IS PART OF PROCESSING TIME

Never try to hurry the cooling process. Food continues to cook during this time and is built into the recipe timing.

Don't place canners in cold spots or in cold water to cool. This may break jars or ruin the canner.

Jars should sit in water-bath canners for at least 5 minutes after boiling has stopped.

Wait 10 minutes after the dial reads zero, or the lid safety lock is released, before removing jars from pressure canners.

CAREFULLY REMOVE JARS

Jars and the canning water will still be hot when you remove jars, so use caution.

You may be able to use hot pads to remove jars from pressure canners, but you will need a jar lifter for water-bath canners.

The jar lifter grips go right under the screw band. Don't try to lift jars by gripping farther down the sides.

Lift jars straight up; try not to tilt or jostle them. They will be wet and slippery.

Home-canned goods should be stored in a cool, dry, dark spot. The temperature should not go above 85°F or below freezing. While they may look beautiful, jars of canned food shouldn't be stored where sunlight shines on them. This could heat the contents and cause seals to break or cause discoloration.

As you can batches, rotate the oldest food in storage to the front of the cupboard so you use that first. Dust and examine stored food every few weeks. Canned food is heavy, so make sure your shelves are sturdy and won't collapse into a disastrous mess.

Important

Wash all jars, especially the lids, before opening them for use. If stored jars have been in contact with floodwater, exposed to leaky sewer pipes, or in a house fire they should be discarded. If jars have been frozen, examine them carefully for cracks, bulging lids, or loose lids and discard damaged jars. In this case, the food could be discarded if the jars are undamaged, and the jars can be sterilized for reuse.

COOLING JARS

Wipe off water and any boiled-over food and place hot jars on cloths or racks to keep cold surfaces from cracking them.

Jars should have at least an inch of space between them or from a wall.

Make sure jars are not in a cold draft but don't cover them.

Don't tighten screw bands after you take jars from the canner. Don't push on the jar lid until the jars feel cool.

REMOVING RIMS AND TESTING SEALS

As jars sit and cool, you may hear a pop as the jars seal. Jars will seal at various times.

After the jars feel cool to the touch (up to 24 hours), remove the screw bands.

The center of the lid should look sucked in if the jar sealed. Pushing on the lid won't show any movement.

The jar will sound a clear ring if the lid is tapped gently with a spoon. If sealed, label and store jars.

PICKLING SUPPLIES

PICKLES CAN BE FERMENTED FIRST OR MADE DURING CANNING; THESE SUPPLIES WILL HELP YOU EITHER WAY

One of the most important supplies for good pickles is the water. Both hard water and chlorinated water can make poor pickles. If your water is hard, buy bottled drinking or distilled water. If your water is chlorinated, fill containers with water and allow them to sit for 48 hours; the chlorine will dissipate.

Use young, fresh, crisp vegetables for pickling. Keep the vegetables chilled until you use them. If you buy vegetables, make sure they are not waxed.

Some pickles are fermented in crocks for several weeks before they are canned. Such pickles used to be kept in those same crocks after fermenting

PICKLE EQUIPMENT FOR FERMENTING

Metals react with the fermenting solution, so fermenting containers should be ceramic, glass, wood, or food-grade plastic.

Lids need to fit down inside the containers, directly on the food to keep it under the brine.

Lids can be plastic, glass, wood, or ceramic, held down with jars of water or doubled food-grade plastic bags filled with brine to keep the food under the brine.

Most fermented food requires a water-bath canner, jars, and lids.

NATURAL FLAVORING

Dill is most commonly associated with pickles, and the flavor can come from flowers, leaves, or seeds.

In pickling, spices are often left whole; sometimes they are added to individual jars or to a brine solution.

Always use pickling or canning salt when making pickles. Other types may cause soft pickles or cloudy brine.

Vinegar used in pickles is both a preservative and a flavor. Don't alter the amount of vinegar in recipes and always use 5 percent acidity vinegar.

finished, but it is now considered safer to can pickles for long-term storage.

Other pickles, called fresh-pack or quick-process pickles, are made right in the canning jar. For the best flavor, these pickles should be left sitting for several weeks before they are eaten. Most recipes in this book are for these kinds of pickles, as they take less time and mess.

Most pickles can be canned in a water-bath canner because they are highly acidic. Some recipes call for pickles to be packed in sterilized jars.

Cucumber Varieties

Some cucumbers make better pickles than others. Pickling-type cucumbers are shorter and fatter when mature and have thinner skins than slicing cucumbers. They are lighter in color on the side away from the sun. Many have bumps on the skin and black spines. Common varieties include Pioneer, Alibi, National Pickling, Liberty, and County Fair.

PREPACKAGED FLAVORING

If you do small amounts of pickle making, then pre-mixed spice packs may work for you. You won't have to spend as much as on individual spices.

Read the label directions for what type of fluid and how much to mix with the package.

All bread-and-butter pickle mixes (or other flavors) don't taste the same, so try small batches first.

Throw away open spice mixes after a year and check the expiration date on sealed packages.

PREPARING FOOD FOR PICKLING

For whole pickles, spears, or slices, use pickling-type cucumbers. Use slicing cucumbers in relishes.

Always slice ¼ inch off the blossom end of the cucumber and discard it. This is the end opposite the stem.

Food-grade lime is used in some recipes to make pickles crisper. There are other packaged products you can add that will firm pickles.

Some vegetables are soaked in ice water or salted before they're used. Follow the recipe for soaking times.

PICKLING BY FERMENTATION

FERMENTATION TURNS VEGETABLES INTO FLAVORFUL SNACKS AND SIDE DISHES

Fermentation gives food a slightly different taste than that of pickles made by the quick-process method. Food has a sour, sharp taste when it has been fermented. The sourness can be adjusted by how long the food is left to ferment.

Fermenting can only be done in a narrow range of temperatures, with 70°F to 75°F the best range. At those temperatures, food is fully fermented in about 3 weeks. Lower temperatures take longer; at 55°F, foods stop fermenting, and at 80°F, pickles usually spoil rather than ferment.

Fermentation produces lactic acid, which preserves the food and changes its color, flavor, and texture. The lactic acid and helpful bacteria form a scum on

COMMONLY FERMENTED FOODS

Not all foods taste good fermented. Fermentation is also called brining. This process leaves food very salty.

Cucumbers and cabbage are the most commonly fermented foods.

Green beans and turnips are occasionally fermented as well, as are a few other vegetables.

Fermentation gives pickles a sharper flavor than fresh-packed pickles. Lactic acid from fermentation also changes the color and texture of foods.

PACKING THE CROCK

For every 5 pounds of produce to ferment you will need a gallon of container space. A 5-gallon container should hold 25 pounds of fermenting produce.

Wash the container with hot, soapy water, rinse with boiling water, and dry with paper towels.

Prepare vegetables and weigh them. The weight determines how much brine solution to make.

Shredded cabbage is generally packed firmly into containers; other vegetables are loosely packed. Leave 5 to 6 inches of space at the top of the containers.

top of the food that should be removed every couple days. If food is fermenting, you will notice gas bubbles under the scum layer.

When you no longer notice bubbles and scum ceases to form, fermentation is finished. Food can be removed after a week of fermentation if you like it less sour.

Cucumbers that have been successfully turned into pickles by fermentation will be crisp and olive green and the insides will be translucent rather than white. Cabbage will be translucent, yellowish, and crisp.

After fermentation, food should be canned and processed in a water-bath canner or placed in fresh brine and refrigerated.

Important

If the container gives off a bad smell (not a yeasty odor), if the food looks slimy or mushy, or if the brine is clear and there is no sign of scum, fermentation either didn't happen or the food spoiled and should be discarded. Any food that has been partially out of the brine also should be discarded. Don't taste food that doesn't look or smell right.

ADDING PICKLING BRINE

A general brine ratio is ½ cup canning salt, ¼ cup vinegar, and 2 quarts water. Spices are added to this per the recipe.

Bring brine to a boil, then cool to room temperature. Hot brine poured in the container will kill good bacteria as well as bad.

Foods should be totally covered with 2 inches of brine.

As fermentation proceeds, you may need to add more brine to keep it 2 inches over the food.

CURING

Fermentation containers should be in an undisturbed spot, above 55°F and below 80°F. Ideal temperature is 70°F.

Food must be below the brine at all times. To keep food from floating up use lids held down with jars or doubled food-grade bags filled with brine.

Fermentation produces a scum layer on top of the container that should be skimmed off every few days.

Fermentation is complete in 3 to 6 weeks, when a scum layer ceases and bubbling stops.

QUICK-PROCESS PICKLES

QUICK-PROCESS PICKLES CAN BE CANNED FOR STORAGE OR STORED IN THE REFRIGERATOR

Quick-process pickles are also called fresh pack. They are made by covering foods with hot brine or syrup and then canning them. Most of the recipes in this book are for quick-process pickles and relishes because they are easier and safer than fermented pickles.

Some quick-process pickle recipes do call for overnight or 24-hour soaking in ice water or a brine solution to make crisper pickles.

Most recipes are canned for storage, but a few may call for refrigeration or freezing. And most pickles and relishes will have a better taste if they are canned

Some Pickle Problems

If you are unsure whether your pickled produce is safe to eat, contact a canning expert. See Chapter 20 for resources.

Pickles are not crisp
    Brine too weak
    Used slicing cucumbers
    Did not remove blossom end of cucumber
    Cooked or processed too long

Shriveled pickles
    Produce not fresh
    Brine or syrup too strong
    Cooked or processed too long

Bitter or off taste
    Used too many or wrong spices or too
        much vinegar
    Dry weather caused bitter fresh produce

Off color
    Used hard water
    Used powdered spices or iodized salt
    Odd reactions of enzymes in the food

QUICK-PROCESS PICKLED FOODS

Besides cucumbers, many types of vegetables and fruits can be pickled. Quick-process pickling allows you to make small batches as produce is available.

Pickling is a good way to use vegetables and fruit that are still green at the end of the season. Green tomatoes make excellent pickles.

Overripe yellow cucumbers and large zucchini can also be pickled.

Small amounts of various vegetables and fruits can be mixed and turned into chutneys and relishes.

and left to sit for a few weeks before being eaten.

Many kinds of vegetables and even fruits are pickled or made into relishes by the quick-process method. But since most of them are made acidic by the pickling ingredients, they are commonly processed in water-bath canners. Processing time will vary according to the foods and jar size, so follow recipe directions.

There are recipes for low-salt and low-sugar pickles and relishes, but don't alter recipes on your own. Don't use artificial sweeteners or salt substitutes unless you have a recipe that calls for them.

Grape Leaves

Grape leaves have an enzyme that makes pickles a bit crisper, and some recipes call for them. You can use fresh wild or garden grape leaves as long as they aren't sprayed with pesticides. To preserve leaves for later canning, wash and dry them, layer them in a nonmetallic container with canning salt between each layer, and then totally cover them. Rinse before use.

BRINING AND PROCESSING

In cold-process pickling, vegetables are generally prepared according to the recipe, then packed into clean jars.

Pint or half-pint jars are usually used for small pickles and relishes, quart-size jars for large cucumbers.

Some recipes call for spices, dill flowers, or other things to be added to each jar.

Brine or syrup is heated to boiling and then poured over the pickles. They are then processed in a water-bath canner for the time specified in the recipe.

REFRIGERATOR PICKLES

Almost any quick-process pickle or relish recipe can be made and then refrigerated instead of canned for storage.

There are special recipes that are meant to be refrigerated for storage, however, and these are best to use if you choose this method.

Taste and crispness of the food may be slightly different in refrigerator pickles and relishes than in canned.

Refrigerator pickles and relishes are meant to be used up quickly, so don't make too much at a time.

FREEZING SUPPLIES

FREEZING IS A QUICK AND EASY ALTERNATIVE TO CANNING FOOD FOR STORAGE

While not everything can be frozen satisfactorily, many foods taste better and maintain their vitamin content better when frozen than when canned or dried.

Freezing is quick, simple, and safe. Modern freezers are energy efficient and relatively modest in cost compared to other large appliances. However, they do cost more than caning supplies, and there is an ongoing cost associated with storing the food because of the electricity used.

That said, your home should not be without a freezer if you are interested in storing some of your food supply. If space is at a premium, think outside the kitchen for a place to locate a freezer. It could be a

FREEZING SUPPLIES

Use freezer bags, not storage bags, for freezing, and use food-grade plastic bags, not garbage bags or recycled bread bags.

Hard-sided containers are better for liquid foods. Make sure they are food-grade plastic or freezer-safe glass with good lids.

Butcher or freezer paper needs special freezer tape to seal it. Don't use regular waxed paper, parchment paper, newspaper, or other papers.

Several small packages freeze better than one large one.

VACUUM SEALING

There are several easy-to-use and inexpensive vacuum sealers on the market today.

Vacuum sealers suck air out of the bag and then use heat to make a tight seal. They help prevent freezer burn and keep food quality high.

Buy freezer, not storage, bags for your type of sealer and follow instructions.

Sealed bags that thaw and warm to above 40°F can develop botulism, since the vacuum removes oxygen. Thaw bags in the refrigerator and use or cook as soon as thawed.

spare room or closet or the basement, laundry room, or porch. The place should stay above freezing but not get too hot, such as in an attic or in the direct sun.

Size your freezer by your family size and what you intend to freeze. If you are raising your own meat, such as a steer or hog, you'll need a large freezer regardless of your family size; you may even need two!

Each cubic foot of freezer space stores about 35 pounds of food. For families that don't raise their meat, 5 to 6 cubic feet of freezer space per person is recommended.

FREEZER CARE

Cool food before placing it in the freezer, and don't try to freeze too much food at one time.

Usually 2 to 3 pounds of food per cubic foot of freezer space is safe to freeze in 24 hours, but check your manual.

Defrost manual-defrost freezers when ¼ inch of frost has built up.

Keep the temperature set at 0°F or below. An open container of baking soda will help absorb any odors.

LABEL AND ROTATE

It's extremely important to label and date food put in the freezer. It's often hard to determine what's in a package after it's frozen.

Regular labels may not stick in the freezer, so use freezer labels or mark the package itself.

While food will be safe in the freezer for a long time, quality and flavor decline over time.

Rotate older food to the front and top of the freezer, where it's easily seen and used first.

FREEZING TECHNIQUES

FOR BEST TASTE, LEARN TO PROPERLY PACKAGE AND MANAGE FOOD IN A FREEZER

Food needs to be packaged properly for the freezer in order to hold its quality and taste for the maximum time. Air is the culprit in freezer burn, a drying out of the food that badly affects food flavor and texture. So in packaging food for the freezer, make every effort to exclude air.

Some space will need to be left at the top of rigid-walled containers to allow for the expansion of food as it freezes; for other packages the goal is no space for air.

Remember the quality of food can only be as good as it was when you froze it. Freezing doesn't kill the

Safe Freezer Storage Times

2–3 months	4–6 months	1 year
Biscuits	Cakes, cookies	Candy
Quick breads	Yeast breads	Poultry
Fruit pies	Meat pies	Beef cuts
Cooked meat	Stews and soups	Lamb
Ground raw meats	Sauces with meat	Fruits except citrus
Shellfish	Citrus fruits and juices	Most vegetables
Milk	Butter	Prepared eggs
Bacon	Raw fish	
Ham	Pork	
	Wild game	

PROPERLY WRAPPING MEAT

Raw meat can be wrapped in freezer paper or packed in plastic bags or vacuum-sealed bags.

Package one meal's worth of meat or the amount you prefer to cook at one time.

Separate pieces enclosed in one package with pieces of freezer paper. Flat packages freeze faster than bulky ones and thaw faster, too.

Try to exclude as much air as possible from packages. Push air out of bags and smooth paper down on meat surfaces.

microorganisms that cause food spoilage; it just stops their growth until the food is thawed. Freezing spoiled meat, for example, will not make it safe to eat. Freeze food as rapidly as possible for the best quality. Try to place packages to be frozen against the freezer walls or shelves in the coldest part of the freezer. You may want to turn the temperature to below 0°F for a day.

No matter how you package them, some foods don't freeze well. Leafy greens and vegetables with a high water content usually don't freeze well when fresh. Other foods freeze well only when specially treated.

CONTAINER FREEZING

Foods with fluid and juices freeze best in rigid containers. Make sure containers are meant for freezing.

Wash containers with hot, soapy water and rinse well before filling.

Some foods expand as they freeze and need space left between the food and the lid. Glass containers need the most space, because expansion may crack them.

Use containers that hold the normal amount of food used in a recipe. Label the container with the amount of food inside, as well as its name and date.

TRAY FREEZING

Some foods stick together when frozen and make thawing and using them difficult.

Spread berries and small pieces of fruit on cookie sheets in a single layer. Cover with plastic wrap and freeze.

When frozen, these foods can be put into bags or containers and they won't stick together. You can quickly remove just what you need.

Frosted cakes or cookies can also be frozen on trays so the frosting won't stick to bags or containers.

FOOD DRYING

DRYING FOOD IS AN ANCIENT WAY OF PRESERVING IT; MODERN EQUIPMENT MAKES IT EASIER

Drying food has had a resurgence of popularity due to handy home-size dehydrators that are now on the market. Although this book has included recipes for sun drying and oven drying, drying food with a dehydrator is the safest and easiest way to do it.

When you dry food, you remove the moisture from it, which inhibits the growth of bacteria, yeasts, and other organisms that spoil food. Properly stored dried food remains good for 6 months to a year or longer.

Dried food is true emergency food, easy to carry and store. While some dried foods, like jerky and fruit leathers, are eaten as is, many dried foods must be

FOOD DEHYDRATORS

A good dehydrator has an adjustable thermostat, a timer that stops the drying, and easy-to-clean removable trays.

If the fan is located on a side or on the back of the dehydrator, the flavors of different foods will be less likely to blend than if it's located at the top or bottom of the unit.

Round dehydrators generally have less usable space because there is a hole in the center of each tray.

Some models have trays that need to be rotated during drying.

SUN DRYING FOOD

To successfully dry food outside, the temperature needs to be above 80°F and the humidity lower than 60 percent for several days.

If your area gets heavy dews, food will have to be covered or brought inside each night.

Screens for holding food should be fiberglass, stainless steel, or plastic. Do not use galvanized mesh. Screens should be raised off the ground.

Food should be covered with cheesecloth, garden row cover, or another screen to keep insects out.

rehydrated before they can be used. So when considering these foods for emergency rations, make sure clean water will also be available.

Commercially dried food often has added sulfur and other preservatives. Sulfite dips can sometimes be purchased wherever winemaking or canning supplies are sold or can be ordered by mail. Follow label directions for their use.

Some foods may need to be treated with color preservatives or blanched before drying. Honey gives dried fruit more calories, but a honey dip is used with many dried fruits as a pretreatment.

OVEN DRYING FOOD

For oven drying, your oven must have a setting of 140°F. You also need an oven thermometer.

To allow moisture to escape, the door must be propped open a few inches. A fan near the open door helps move moisture away.

Watch the oven thermometer and adjust heat to keep it at 140°F. Oven drying can take 24 hours or more.

Convection ovens make better dryers if they have a low heat setting because there is built-in air movement.

STORING DRIED FOODS

Dried foods must be stored so that they don't pick up moisture from the air.

Dried food must cool before it's packaged. Fruit needs to be conditioned before final packaging. Loosely fill jars with fruit and shake or stir daily for 10 days.

Vacuum sealers work well to store dried food. Glass or plastic containers with tight lids can be used as well.

Storing tightly wrapped foods in the refrigerator or freezer prolongs their storage life. Always label and date packages.

PEACHES IN SYRUP

SUN-RIPENED PEACHES CAPTURED AT THEIR JUICIEST MAKE DELIGHTFUL WINTER EATING

Ripe peaches do not store for very long, so canning them at their peak of ripeness allows you to savor that juicy taste for much longer. Choose peaches that are fully tree ripened but that don't have large bruises or soft spots.

Peaches are best when canned in syrup; this recipe calls for medium-heavy syrup. You can reduce the amount of sugar or can the peaches in water or juice. See recipe variations. Do not use artificial sweeteners.

Freestone peaches slip easily from their pits and golden-fleshed peaches make prettier jars than their lighter-fleshed relatives. Special peach peelers can make removing the soft fuzzy skin easier. *Yield: 7 quarts*

What You Will Need

17 ½ pounds peaches

Color preservative solution: ½ cup lemon juice mixed with ½ gallon water or ascorbic acid per label directions

5 cups white sugar

8 cups water

7 clean, hot quart jars and lids

Water-bath canner

PEACHES IN SYRUP

Bring a large pot of water to a simmer. Prepare a pot of cold water. Dip peaches in the hot water 1 minute, then dip in the cold water; slip off the skins and discard.

Slice peaches in half; remove pits. Place in mixture of lemon juice or ascorbic acid and water until you are ready to cook, then drain.

Bring sugar and water to a boil. Add drained peaches. Bring to boil. Turn off heat.

Ladle peaches and syrup into hot jars, cut side down, to ½ inch from rim. Remove bubbles, wipe rims, put on lids, and process.

Water-Bath Canner Processing Times for Quarts				
Altitude in Feet	0-1,000	1,001-3,000	3,001-6,000	6,001+
Processing Time	25 minutes	30 minutes	35 minutes	40 minutes

PRECOOKING

Peaches are precooked to inactivate enzymes that cause discoloration and softness.

Be careful not to overcook, or your peaches will get mushy when processed.

The sugar and water should be vigorously boiling when you add the peaches. Slide the peaches in carefully so hot fluid doesn't splash up on your hands.

Keep a close watch, and as soon as the fluid is boiling again, shut off the heat.

FILLING JARS

You could actually slice or dice the peaches, but halves look so much prettier in the jars.

Turning the cut sides down and nestling halves on top of each other is the best use of space, and it looks nicer, too.

If the halves are small, you can tuck some halves along the jar sides, cut side in.

Make sure to run a bubble stick through the filled jars before placing the lids. Peach halves can trap air in their hollows.

PEARS IN JUICE
MANY OTHER FRUITS CAN ALSO BE CANNED IN JUICE

Pears are the odd fruit that actually ripen best off the tree. When pears get their mature color, which can be yellow, green, brown, or red, they are picked and allowed to soften for a few days. Asian pears are round like apples and never get as soft as regular pears.

Bartlett pears are top canning pears, but many other varieties are also good. Tiny canned Seckel pears make attractive garnishes or additions to salads. Choose pears that are just softening, without large bruises or soft spots, for canning. It takes about 2½ pounds of whole pears to make each quart of canned pears.

Pears contain the sweetest natural sugar, levulose, in a higher concentration than any other fruit. *Yield: 7 quarts*

What You Will Need

17½ pounds pears

Color preservative solution: ½ cup lemon juice mixed with ½ gallon water or ascorbic acid per label directions

1 gallon apple juice (not cider)

7 clean, hot quart jars and lids

Water-bath canner

PEARS IN JUICE

Wash and peel pears, slice lengthwise, and use melon baller to core; cut into slices.

Put pear slices in a pot with color preservative solution while heating juice.

Bring apple juice to a boil. Drain pears in colander and add. Boil 5 minutes. Turn off heat.

Ladle sliced pears and juice into hot jars to ½ inch from top, remove bubbles, wipe rim, place lids, and process.

Water-Bath Canner Processing Times for Quarts				
Altitude in Feet	0-1,000	1,001-3,000	3,001-6,000	6,001+
Processing Time	25 minutes	30 minutes	35 minutes	40 minutes

Carmelized Pears

Drain and chill canned pears. Save juice. Pour 2 tablespoons caramel ice-cream sauce into saucer; add ½ cup pear slices. Heat ½ cup canned pear juice with 2 teaspoons brown sugar, 1 teaspoon butter, and ⅛ teaspoon cinnamon until bubbly; pour over pear slices. Drizzle more caramel sauce over pears, sprinkle with chopped walnuts. Add whipped cream. *Yield: 1 serving*

CORING PEARS

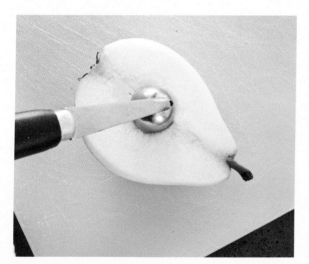

Pears can be peeled with a potato peeler or a paring knife. Slice them lengthwise.

To easily remove the core, run a melon baller or small spoon down the middle to scrape out the tough membrane and seeds.

Pears are odd shaped and may look better sliced than halved, and slices may fit into jars better than halves.

Pears darken when exposed to air, so slip them into the color preservative solution as each is sliced.

FILLING JARS

Because pears are firm, dense fruits, they are precooked for 5 minutes in boiling juice before packed into jars.

Once precooking is complete, ladle hot pears into jars right away.

Try to get equal amounts of pear slices and juice into each jar. Fill jars with hot juice up to ½ inch from the jar rim.

Unsweetened white grape juice or pineapple juice can be substituted for the apple juice.

CITRUS IN WATER
THIS RECIPE IS THE LOWEST-CALORIE VERSION OF CANNED FRUIT AND CAN BE ADAPTED FOR MANY FRUITS

If you are lucky enough to live in a warm area of the United States, you may have orange trees in the back yard instead of apple or peach trees. Or you may have grapefruit, lime, or lemon trees.

Like other fruits, citrus can be canned when it is abundant and used at other times of the year. This is the lowest-calorie version of canned fruit, as it is canned in water. Most fruits can be canned in a similar manner. Citrus can also be canned in juice or sugar syrup.

Choose citrus fruits that are fully ripe for canning. The best way to know if they are ripe is to taste them. The fruit should have no large bruises.

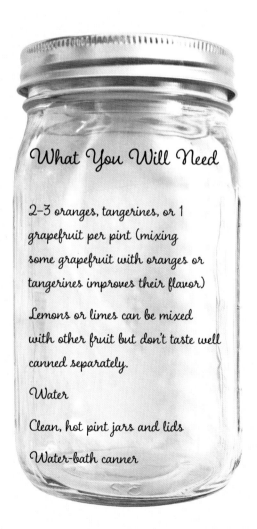

What You Will Need

2–3 oranges, tangerines, or 1 grapefruit per pint (mixing some grapefruit with oranges or tangerines improves their flavor)

Lemons or limes can be mixed with other fruit but don't taste well canned separately.

Water

Clean, hot pint jars and lids

Water-bath canner

CITRUS IN WATER

Wash citrus in warm water. Remove all peels. Remove all the white fibrous material (albedo) on the outside of the fruit.

Section the citrus or cut lemons and limes into rounds. Bring water to a boil, about 1 cup per pint.

Fill jars loosely with fruit. Don't compress or squeeze. Leave ½ inch to rim.

Pour boiling water over fruit to fill spaces and cover fruit. Remove bubbles, wipe rims add lids, and process.

Water-Bath Canner Processing Times for Pints or Quarts				
Altitude in Feet	0-1,000	1,001-3,000	3,001-6,000	6,001+
Processing Time	10 minutes	15 minutes	15 minutes	20 minutes

Recipe Variation

To keep the calories down or to avoid white sugar, most fruits can be canned in water. Pears, cherries, plums, and most berries can be canned in water. Apples, peaches, and grapes keep their color and texture better in juice or syrup but can also be canned in water. Cranberries should be canned in syrup. To can in water, prepare the fruit and substitute water for syrup or juice.

PREPARING CITRUS FRUIT

Wash the outer peel well before peeling. Remove the entire peel. Pull fruit sections apart.

The white, stringy fibrous material on the inner surface needs to be carefully picked off. It creates a bitter taste when canned.

Use a knife or scissors to trim off the middle, fibrous area— where the seeds are—and remove as many seeds as possible.

Large grapefruit sections can be cut in half. Lemons and limes should be sliced into rounds instead of sectioned.

FILLING JARS

Pack jars loosely with the fruit sections or rounds to about the jars' shoulders. Leave ½-inch headspace.

Don't compress or mash the fruit. Shaking the jars lightly may provide extra room.

If more than one fruit is used, try to arrange equal amounts in each jar. Blood oranges and red grapefruit add color.

Boiling water must cover all the fruit before processing. After removing bubbles, add more water if needed.

CHERRIES IN SYRUP

CHERRIES MAY BE HARD TO PIT, BUT THEY MAKE A WIDE RANGE OF TASTY DISHES

There are sweet dessert-type cherries and tart cherries, and both can equally well. Choose cherries that are fully ripe and don't hold onto them long before canning.

Tart cherries are generally red, but sweet cherries range from deep red-black to yellow. Heavily bruised, moldy, or bird-damaged cherries should be discarded.

Sometimes cherries are canned with their pits, but to make them recipe ready, most cherries are pitted before canning. If they are not pitted, cherries must have their skin pricked before processing to keep them from bursting.

What You Will Need

11 pounds cherries

Color preservative solution: ½ cup lemon juice mixed with ½ gallon water or ascorbic acid per label directions

5½ cups water and 2½ cups sugar (for sweet cherries) or 5 cups water and 3¼ cups sugar (for sour cherries)

9 clean, hot pint jars and lids

Water-bath canner

CHERRIES IN SYRUP

Wash cherries, remove stems, and pit them.

Place cherries in color preservative solution while you bring the water to boil.

Combine sugar and water and bring to a boil; add drained cherries, return to boil, and turn off heat.

Ladle cherries and syrup into jars to ½ inch from rim. Remove bubbles, wipe rim, add lids, and process.

Cherries are high in antioxidants and have many health benefits associated with them. *Yield: 9 pints*

Water-Bath Canner Processing Times for Pints				
Altitude in Feet	0-1,000	1,001-3,000	3,001-6,000	6,001+
Processing Time	15 minutes	20 minutes	20 minutes	25 minutes

MAKE IT EASY

Single cherry pitters are very inexpensive. (An olive pitter works, too.) If you can't find one, use the tip of a potato peeler, a small crochet hook, or a nut pick to scrape the pit out. Or use a piece of rigid plastic drinking straw (the reusable kind) to push the pit through the cherry. You can also pull the cherry apart, but those cherries don't look as nice.

PITTING CHERRIES

Pitting cherries is messy work no matter how you do it. Cherry juice stains, so wear an apron or old clothes.

If you don't have a cherry pitter, see the tips in the sidebar for homemade tools.

The stem end of pitted cherries will discolor, so as you pit cherries pop them in the color preservative solution.

Half-frozen cherries are easier to pit and are less messy. Set small batches in the freezer for 30 minutes before pitting.

FILLING JARS

Do not cook cherries too long, or they will lose their color and shape; the syrup and cherries need to be brought to just boiling.

You can add a few drops of red food coloring to the cherries before filling the jars if desired.

Try to get equal amounts of cherries and syrup in each jar.

Cherries tend to settle to the bottom if there is too much syrup; if necessary use one less jar so jars look filled.

MIXED FRUIT IN SYRUP

USUALLY KNOWN AS FRUIT COCKTAIL, THIS DISH IS ESPECIALLY POPULAR WITH KIDS

Mixed Fruit in Syrup can be a fun dish for kids or an elegant dessert for guests, depending on the fruits used and the presentation. Consider using some exotic fruits like papaya or star fruit with the common fruits from your garden to make your mixed fruit more exciting. Mixed Fruit in Syrup is also a way to use up small batches of fruit. When using citrus, remove all white tissue from sections.

Usually the fruit for this recipe is cut into small cubes, but you can be creative. It takes 12 cups of peeled and diced fruit to make about 6 pints of mixed fruit. Try to make the blend colorful. Pint jars

What You Will Need

8 pounds diced fruit, your choice of varieties (see suggested blends)

Color preservative solution: ½ cup lemon juice mixed with ½ gallon water or ascorbic acid per label directions

3 cups sugar

4 cups water

6 hot, clean pint jars and lids

1 10-ounce jar maraschino cherries (optional)

Water-bath canner

MIXED FRUIT IN SYRUP

Wash, peel, and dice fruit into ½-inch cubes. Leave grapes whole. Place fruit in color preservative solution.

Combine sugar and water in a pot, bring to a boil, and turn off heat.

Pour ½ cup hot syrup into each jar, then drain fruit and add to near top of jar. Push a few maraschino cherries into each jar with a bubble stick.

Fill any space with more syrup to ½ inch from rim, remove bubbles, wipe rim, top with lids, and process.

are recommended. You can also can mixed fruit in apple, white grape, or pineapple juice. *Yield: 6 pints*

Water-Bath Canner Processing Times for Pints				
Altitude in Feet	0-1,000	1,001-3,000	3,001-6,000	6,001+
Processing Time	20 minutes	25 minutes	30 minutes	35 minutes

Recipe Variation

American: whole seedless green grapes, peaches, pears, pineapple; **Tropical:** red seedless grapes, pineapple, papaya, tangerine sections, pears; **Exotic:** star fruit, pineapple, kiwi slices, papaya, whole blackberries, apricots; **Patriotic:** red seedless grapes, red maraschino cherries, pears, large whole blueberries; **Holiday:** red tart cherries, green seedless grapes, pears, raspberries, kiwi slices

PREPARING FRUIT

Don't wash fruit until just before using. Purchased fruits should be washed well and any wax removed with warm, soapy water. Rinse well.

Each type of fruit needs to be peeled and sliced or diced into bite-size pieces.

Grapes can be cut in half if they have seeds and the seeds removed. Seedless grapes can be left whole.

Larger firm fruits like pears and peaches should be used in larger amounts than grapes and berries in the mixes.

ADDING COLOR

Canned commercial maraschino cherries in red or green can be added to make fruit mixes more attractive. Don't use more than 2 to 3 per jar.

Think about the colors of fruit when blending fruits and strive for a mixture of colors.

Dark red tart cherries, blueberries, and blackberries can be used in small amounts for color.

Push your color accents into filled jars along the sides so the jars look attractive.

SPICED APPLE RINGS
SOMETHING A LITTLE DIFFERENT, BOTH PRETTY AND TASTY

Apples can be canned plain in juice, water, or syrup, but they hold their texture better in syrup. And plain canned apples can be rather bland. This recipe brings a snap to them. Remember to choose firm, small apples about 2½ inches in diameter so your rings will fit in the jars.

This unusual and fun recipe uses a common candy often called Red Hots. They are usually shaped like hearts but may also be round or oblong. They have a strong, fiery cinnamon flavor that combines well with apples.

You can vary this recipe by using pear slices or small Seckel pears cut in half. Small crabapples can be cored and left whole as well. *Yield: 9 pints*

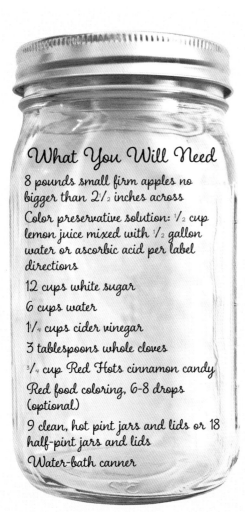

What You Will Need

8 pounds small firm apples no bigger than 2½ inches across

Color preservative solution: ½ cup lemon juice mixed with ½ gallon water or ascorbic acid per label directions

12 cups white sugar

6 cups water

1¼ cups cider vinegar

3 tablespoons whole cloves

¾ cup Red Hots cinnamon candy

Red food coloring, 6-8 drops (optional)

9 clean, hot pint jars and lids or 18 half-pint jars and lids

Water-bath canner

SPICED APPLE RINGS

Wash apples. Then peel, core, and slice into ½-inch rounds; place in color preservative solution until ready to cook.

Combine sugar, water, vinegar, and cloves in a large pot and bring to a boil; add Red Hots and food coloring (optional).

Simmer and stir 3 minutes, until candy dissolves. Drain apples in colander and add. Cook 5 minutes. Turn off heat.

Transfer rings to jars; pour hot syrup over to ½ inch from rim. Wipe rim, top with lids, and process.

Water-Bath Canner Processing Times for Pints or Half-Pints				
Altitude in Feet	0-1,000	1,001-3,000	3,001-6,000	6,001+
Processing Time	10 minutes	15 minutes	15 minutes	20 minutes

SLICING APPLES

After peeling, use a knife or coring tool to remove the core where the stiff membrane and seeds are located.

Turn the apple on its side and carefully slice it into ½-inch rings. Immediately place the slices into color preservative solution.

The spices and candy will change the apple color, so you can omit the color preservative solution, which will result in darker rings.

Widemouthed jars accommodate larger apple rings. Slightly large rings can be bent to fit through jar openings.

CANDY ADDS FLAVOR

The candies give the rings color and a spicy hot flavor. You can also substitute 8 cinnamon sticks and red food coloring for the candy.

Keep the water hot, but don't allow it to boil as you stir the candies to dissolve them.

Watch the apples carefully as they simmer in the candy mixture. Don't let them stick to the bottom or sides of the pot.

To fill jars, gently lift the rings with tongs or a slotted spoon so they don't break.

APPLE PIE FILLING

THIS RECIPE WORKS WELL WITH PEACHES, TOO

There is nothing better than hot apple pie. And having the filling ready to use makes it quick and easy to prepare. Apple Pie Filling can be used to make numerous other desserts, too.

Before the Clear Jel product used in this recipe was developed, pie fillings needed to be thickened just before the pie was made. Other thickeners break down under the heat used when processing the jars.

Because apples vary in flavor, you may want to adjust the sugar slightly or add more lemon juice to suit your taste. You can also modify the spices.

This recipe makes a filling that looks just like commercially canned filling. It also works well with fresh peaches and can be frozen as well as canned. *Yield: 7 quarts*

APPLE PIE FILLING

What You Will Need

16 pounds apples

Color preservative solution: ½ cup lemon juice mixed with ½ gallon water or ascorbic acid per label directions

Large strainer or colander with handles

5 cups apple juice

5½ cups white sugar

1½ cups Clear Jel

2½ cups water

1 tablespoon cinnamon

1 teaspoon nutmeg

1 teaspoon allspice

¾ cups lemon juice

7 clean, hot quart jars and lids

Water-bath canner

Peel, core, and slice apples. Store in color preservative solution.

Bring water to a boil. Dip batches of apples in a colander into boiling water for 1 minute. Keep blanched apples warm while working.

Place apple juice, sugar, Clear Jel, water, and spices in a pot. Bring to a boil, stirring until thick and bubbly. Add lemon juice; boil 1 minute.

Fold apples into syrup. Ladle into jars to ½ inch from rim. Remove bubbles, wipe rim, top with lids, and process.

Water-Bath Canner Processing Times for Quarts				
Altitude in Feet	0-1,000	1,001-3,000	3,001-6,000	6,001+
Processing Time	25 minutes	30 minutes	35 minutes	40 minutes

Clear Jel

Clear Jel is not always found in regular grocery stores, but specialty cooking stores and food service stores often carry it. There are numerous online and mail-order sources for it, including Amazon. Check Chapter 20 for other resources. One pound of Clear Jel equals about 3 cups. Do not use instant Clear Jel in canning. Jelly and jam thickeners will not give the same results.

BLANCHING APPLES

Blanching is done to remove enzymes that cause peeled fruit to darken when exposed to air. In this recipe it also heats the apples.

Use a colander or strainer to dip small amounts of slices into the boiling water at one time.

The slices need to be warm when added to the filling, so unlike other blanching, do not dip the slices in cold water after boiling.

Keep the slices warm in covered bowls until all are blanched.

FOLDING IN APPLES

The filling is cooked separately so the boiling and stirring don't break down the apple slices and make them too soft.

Lemon juice is added at the end of cooking so the acidity doesn't decrease. A small amount of yellow food coloring can be added to improve color.

Gently work the slices into the syrup to evenly distribute them.

When filling jars, try to get even amounts of filling and fruit into each jar.

PINK APPLESAUCE

APPLESAUCE MAKES A GOOD DESSERT OR SIDE DISH

This is a pretty applesauce with a little added anti-oxidant power. The cherry juice used to color it also gives it a slightly different taste. Children especially enjoy this recipe.

If you don't have cherry juice or don't want the sauce to be pink, simply substitute water for the cherry juice and leave out the food coloring.

Applesauce is used as a side dish in many cultures, as well as a dessert. It goes well with pork dishes.

You can add more or less sugar to the recipe and adjust the spices to suit your taste. Allspice, nutmeg, and cloves are common spices used to flavor apple-sauce. *Yield: 7 quarts*

What You Will Need

20 pounds apples (use a combination of tart and sweet apples for best taste)

1 cup unsweetened cherry juice

1 tablespoon cinnamon (optional)

½ teaspoon red food coloring (optional)

Food processor or blender (optional)

1 cup white sugar

7 clean, hot quart jars and lids

Water-bath canner

PINK APPLESAUCE

Wash, peel, and core apples; chop into 2-inch chunks.

Combine apples, juice, and optional cinnamon and food coloring in a pot. Bring to a simmer, and cook until tender, about 15 minutes. Stir occasionally to prevent burning.

Drain apples, put in food processor, or blender and process to desired consistency (or hand mash). Place sauce in a pot, add sugar, bring to a boil, and turn off heat.

Fill jars to ½ inch from rim, wipe rim, put on lids, and process.

Water-Bath Canner Processing Times for Quarts				
Altitude in Feet	0-1,000	1,001-3,000	3,001-6,000	6,001+
Processing Time	20 minutes	25 minutes	30 minutes	35 minutes

Recipe Variation

To keep the applesauce very light in color, slice apples into a color preservative solution. If you don't use a color preservative and don't add color, it will be darker than commercial applesauce. The applesauce will also be darker and have a slightly different flavor if you use brown sugar instead of white. You can alter the smoothness of the sauce by how well you mash or strain it.

BLENDING APPLES

Make sure to stir apples frequently while they cook. A little burnt area will spread the burnt flavor through the entire pot.

Once apples are cooked, drain off any extra fluid and place the hot apples in the food processor or blender.

Process in short bursts until desired consistency is reached.

The apples can also be blended with a potato masher or large spoon. Mash them in the pot just before you add the sugar.

FILLING JARS

After the apples are blended smooth, put the sauce in a pot, add the sugar, and thoroughly mix.

Then bring the sauce to a boil, stirring constantly so it won't scorch.

As soon as the sauce bubbles on the surface, turn off the heat. Immediately ladle the hot sauce into jars.

Make sure to leave a ½-inch headspace and wipe the rim so the lid will seal.

GREEN TOMATO PIE FILLING

A UNIQUE AND DELICIOUS WAY TO USE THOSE GREEN TOMATOES BEFORE FROST

It seems there are always too many green tomatoes left at the end of the season, and people are always looking for ways to use them. Apples are usually available at the end of tomato season, too, so why not combine the two?

This is a slightly tart but delicious filling for your favorite piecrust. You can vary the spices, but don't alter the lemon juice and vinegar given in this recipe. Green tomatoes lower the acidity of the filling, and the added acidity is necessary for safe water-bath canning.

This is the perfect recipe to use for an autumn picnic or maybe to enter in the county fair. *Yield: 7 quarts*

GREEN TOMATO PIE FILLING

What You Will Need

16 cups green tomatoes, cut into 2-inch slices

12 cups tart apples, peeled, cored, and cut into 2-inch slices

2 pounds golden seedless raisins

2 cups water

2½ cups brown sugar

2½ cups white sugar

1 cup lemon juice

½ cup cider vinegar

2 tablespoons cinnamon

1 tablespoon nutmeg

7 clean, hot quart jars and lids

Water-bath canner

Place all ingredients in a large saucepan.

Bring to a simmer; cook and stir until the fruit is tender and mixture looks slightly thickened, about 40 minutes.

Turn off heat and ladle mixture into hot jars; leave ½-inch headspace.

Remove bubbles, wipe rim, put on lids, and process.

Water-Bath Canner Processing Times for Quarts				
Altitude in Feet	0-1,000	1,001-3,000	3,001-6,000	6,001+
Processing Time	15 minutes	20 minutes	20 minutes	25 minutes

Important

This filling will be thinner than the Apple Pie Filling on page 52 that calls for Clear Jel. Do not try to thicken it with cornstarch or other thickeners before canning. It will result in a poor-looking and -tasting product that may not be safe. You can thicken it just before you use it in your favorite crust if you need to.

PREPARING THE FRUIT

The best tomatoes to use for this recipe are those that are just starting to color but are still be firm. Don't peel the tomatoes.

Remove the stem and hard center core area of the tomatoes and slice into 2-inch thick pieces.

Remove the apple peel, the center core, and seeds. Firm cooking-type apples work best.

There's no need to use color preservative on the apple pieces because the mixture is naturally darker.

COOKING THE FILLING

Everything is put into the saucepan at the same time.

The mixture needs to cook slowly, at just under the boiling point. Stir it frequently to keep it from scorching.

The sugar and the pectin in the apples will thicken the mixture as it slowly cooks.

Some batches will get thicker than others. When the fruit pieces are soft but not falling apart, the mixture is done. Fill jars while the mix is very hot.

CHERRY PIE FILLING OR TOPPING

THIS RECIPE WORKS WELL WITH ALL KINDS OF BERRIES, TOO

While this recipe uses cherries, you could just as easily use blueberries, blackberries, or raspberries for juicy berry pies. If you are making cherry filling or topping, use tart or pie cherries.

This recipe uses Clear Jel, which was used in the Apple Pie Filling recipe. You can get some ideas on where to find it on page 53 or in Chapter 20. Don't try to use other thickeners in this recipe.

To make your filling look more professional, tint it with red food coloring for cherries and a combination of red and blue coloring for other berries.

What You Will Need

6 quarts tart cherries

Large strainer or colander

7 cups white sugar

1³/₄ cup Clear Jel

9¹/₃ cups water

2 teaspoons almond extract

¹/₂ cup concentrated lemon juice

7 clean, hot quart jars and lids

Water-bath canner

CHERRY PIE FILLING OR TOPPING

Wash cherries; remove stems and pits.

Fill a large pot with water and bring to a boil. Fill colander with cherries, lower into water, and leave 1 minute. Remove cherries; keep warm. Repeat with remaining cherries.

In a saucepan, combine sugar, Clear Jel, water, and extract. Cook and stir until thick and bubbly. Add lemon juice; cook 1 minute. Remove from heat.

Fold cherries into syrup and fill jars to ½ inch from rim. Remove bubbles, wipe rims, top with lids, and process.

This filling is an excellent topping for cakes or ice cream, too. *Yield: 7 quarts*

Water-Bath Canner Processing Times for Quarts				
Altitude in Feet	0-1,000	1,001-3,000	3,001-6,000	6,001+
Processing Time	30 minutes	35 minutes	40 minutes	45 minutes

GETTING FILLING TO GEL

Clear Jel is quite easy to use and generally gives you a good gel. Don't use other products to thicken this recipe.

It's important to keep stirring the mix so that it doesn't scorch. When it's thick and bubbly, add the lemon juice.

The lemon juice isn't cooked very long because it would lose its acidity.

The cherries should be warm when you fold them into the filling. Try to distribute them evenly through it.

USING CHERRY FILLING

Open a jar of cherry pie filling and use it to fill prebaked tart shells for a quick cherry dessert.

Use cherry pie filling on chocolate cake instead of frosting; it's sweet but better for you.

Fill a graham cracker crust with vanilla pudding and cherry filling for a quick dessert.

Blend cherry filling until smooth and use it as a barbecue sauce or dipping sauce. Try it as a glaze for roast duck.

CRANBERRY SAUCE

THIS BRIGHT SAUCE IS GREAT FOR THE HOLIDAYS OR AS A GIFT

While cranberries are seldom grown in home gardens, they are showing up more often in local markets as fresh berries. Cranberries are usually grown in North America, but other countries do grow some cranberries.

This recipe is for one of the cranberry's most traditional uses—a sauce generally served with poultry—but feel free to find nontraditional uses for it.

If you like the flavor of orange mixed with cranberries, substitute unsweetened orange juice for the water in this recipe.

This recipe makes a thick sauce, not a jelly-like product. You could strain it through cheesecloth or a jelly bag if you want a more jelly-like texture and look.

Cranberry Sauce is a nice hostess gift at the holidays. **Yield: 6 pints**

What You Will Need

3 pounds raw cranberries

3 cups water

Food sieve or food strainer

6 cups sugar

6 clean, hot pint jars and lids

Water-bath canner

CRANBERRY SAUCE

Wash cranberries. Put water and cranberries in a saucepan and cook on low heat until soft.

Drain cranberries and mash through a food sieve or food strainer. Discard skins and seeds.

Place cranberry pulp in saucepan and add sugar. Bring to a boil; boil 3 minutes.

Ladle hot cranberry sauce into jars, remove bubbles, and wipe rim. Top with lids and process.

Water-Bath Canner Processing Times for Pints				
Altitude in Feet	0-1,000	1,001-3,000	3,001-6,000	6,001+
Processing Time	15 minutes	20 minutes	20 minutes	25 minutes

Cranberry Tips

Native Americans used cranberries for food and medicine, and they were a dish served at peace ceremonies, which may explain why we serve them today at holiday feasts. Cranberries are loaded with vitamins and antioxidants and are good for you. Fresh cranberries should be deep red and firm, not shriveled or soft. Fresh berries will store in a cool place for weeks.

STRAINING CRANBERRIES

Softened cranberries can be put through a food mill or crushed by hand.

To crush, place the berries in a sieve or strainer with small holes and push the pulp through with a wooden spoon or pestle.

Work in small batches. Rinse the sieve or strainer off between batches and discard seeds and skin.

The pulp must be reheated with the sugar before filling the jars.

MAKING THE SAUCE A GIFT

You can use half-pint jars instead of pint jars for small gifts. You can find pretty embossed jars in many stores or online.

Replace the rim with a white storage cap or use brushed platinum lids.

Center a square of pretty fabric over the jar top and tie a contrasting ribbon under the rim.

You can make decorative labels on your computer or purchase them in stores. You can also decorate jars with holiday stickers.

PEACH DIPPING SAUCE

AN INTERESTING DIP OR GLAZE FOR PORK OR CHICKEN

If you are tired of making peach pie and cobbler, why not use some of those fresh peaches to make this interesting sweet-and-sour sauce?

This delicious dipping sauce will have you scouring the kitchen for something to dip. It can also be used to coat pork roast or make a crispy golden glaze on chicken. You can also use this sauce as a substitute for plum sauce with egg rolls.

You can adjust the spices to suit your taste. If children will be enjoying the sauce, you may want to decrease the pepper.

This sauce also freezes well in freezer-safe containers. *Yield: 4 half-pint jars*

What You Will Need

4 cups peeled, chopped, firm but ripe peaches

1 medium onion

1 cup sugar

½ cup white vinegar

¼ teaspoon salt

¼ teaspoon allspice

½ teaspoon cloves

½ teaspoon cinnamon

¼ teaspoon red pepper

4 sterilized half-pint jars and lids

Water-bath canner

PEACH DIPPING SAUCE

To remove peach skins, dip peaches in boiling water, then ice water, and then slip off the skins. Remove pit; chop peaches. Peel and finely dice onion.

Place all ingredients in a large saucepan; slowly bring to a boil. Lower heat and simmer 1 hour, stirring frequently.

Remove from heat and blend until smooth. Return to heat and boil 1 minute, stirring constantly.

Pour hot sauce into jars to ¼ inch from rim, wipe rim, top with lids, and process.

Water-Bath Canner Processing Times for Half-Pints				
Altitude in Feet	0-1,000	1,001-3,000	3,001-6,000	6,001+
Processing Time	5 minutes	10 minutes	10 minutes	15 minutes

PREPARING PEACHES AND ONIONS

Peaches are hard to peel unless you blanch them. Don't leave them in the boiling water too long—count to 60, then plunge into ice water.

After being in the cold water, the skins should slide right off. You may have to cut a bit off near the stem. Work with a few at a time.

Open the peaches, remove the pit, then dice into tiny pieces.

The onion should be finely diced so that when cooked it disappears into the sauce.

BLEND AND REHEAT SAUCE

As the peaches and onions cook, stir frequently to prevent scorching, which causes an off flavor.

If scorching occurs, turn off the heat and transfer the sauce to a clean pan, being careful not to dislodge burnt areas. Begin the cooking again, stirring more frequently.

When the peaches are very soft, use a hand mixer or blender to smooth them into a thick, glossy consistency.

You must bring the sauce to a boil before filling the jars; stir constantly.

STRAWBERRY JAM

TURN A BOUNTIFUL SPRING STRAWBERRY HARVEST INTO A SWEET TREAT THAT LASTS ALL YEAR

The bountiful strawberry harvest generally occurs in early summer before you have tired of trying to preserve things. But if this is a hectic time, you can freeze the strawberries and turn them into jam later.

There's nothing more delicious than Strawberry Jam slathered on toast, unless, of course, it's Strawberry Jam spread on a big flaky biscuit! Strawberry Jam is also good on pound cake or drizzled over a scoop of ice cream.

Jam differs from jelly in that it is thicker and pieces of fruit and seeds can be distinguished in the finished jam. It's very hard to strain out strawberry seeds for jelly, as they are so small. Strawberry Jam can also be frozen. *Yield: 8 half-pint jars*

What You Will Need

16 cups fresh whole strawberries

6 cups white sugar

Candy or jelly thermometer

8 sterilized half-pint jars with lids

Water-bath canner

STRAWBERRY JAM

Wash strawberries and remove stems. Slice in quarters and put in a saucepan. Crush with a potato masher or back of ladle.

Be sure you have 8 cups strawberries and juice. Add sugar. Bring to a boil slowly, stirring constantly until sugar dissolves.

Turn up heat and cook quickly, 35 to 40 minutes, until mix thickens and reaches 220°F; stir often. Turn off heat.

Pour hot jam into sterile jars. Leave ¼-inch headspace. Wipe rim, put on lids, and process.

Water-Bath Canner Processing Times for Half-Pints				
Altitude in Feet	0-1,000	1,001-3,000	3,001-6,000	6,001+
Processing Time	5 minutes	10 minutes	10 minutes	15 minutes

Important

Jams, jellies, and preserves call for sterilized jars. If they are processed longer to kill bacteria, the gel can be lost. Refer to page 17 to find out how to sterilize jars. Until you're ready to use them, jars must be kept submerged in boiling water. If you use a dishwasher with a sterilize setting, keep the jars warm inside the dishwasher until you're ready to use them. Check the lid box to see what sterilization method is recommended.

CRUSHING STRAWBERRIES

Slicing and crushing the strawberries releases the juice, which is needed to dissolve the sugar.

After crushing the strawberries, you must carefully measure out 8 cups of fruit and juice, as the ratio of fruit to sugar determines the gel.

Stir the jam frequently while the sugar is dissolving. Don't let the sugar scorch on the pan.

Place the thermometer in the pot as soon as the jam begins cooking and keep it there.

KNOWING THE JELLING POINT

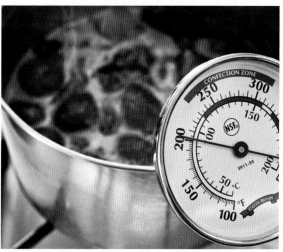

If you have a candy or jelly thermometer, watch it carefully and turn off the heat when the jam temperature reaches 220°F.

If you do not have a thermometer, cook and stir until the jam looks thick and shiny.

Jam will be a bit thicker when it cools. To check the consistency, place a spoonful in the freezer for 5 minutes.

You can continue to cook jam that isn't thick enough, but overcooked jam will get grainy and taste like caramelized sugar.

GRAPE JELLY
WHAT'S A PEANUT BUTTER SANDWICH WITHOUT GRAPE JELLY?

Concord grapes are the premier grapes for making jelly, but any grapes, including wild grapes, can be turned into jelly. A few underripe grapes in the jelly batch increase the natural pectin level and help the jelly to set well.

Jelly making is even more exacting than making jam, but grapes are one of the easiest fruits to turn into jelly. Jelly making also takes time, as it can take hours for the juice to strain through a jelly bag.

Besides making good peanut butter and jelly sandwiches, Grape Jelly can be mixed with chili sauce for a meatball marinade (see Reduced-Sugar Grape Jelly on page 226 for recipe) or used to attract Baltimore orioles to the yard, as they adore a dish of grape jelly.
Yield: 8 half-pint jars

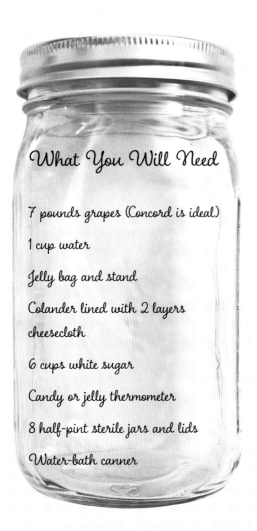

What You Will Need

7 pounds grapes (Concord is ideal)

1 cup water

Jelly bag and stand

Colander lined with 2 layers cheesecloth

6 cups white sugar

Candy or jelly thermometer

8 half-pint sterile jars and lids

Water-bath canner

GRAPE JELLY

Wash grapes, place in pot, and crush. Add water, bring to a boil, reduce heat, and simmer 10 minutes.

Place grapes in jelly bag and collect juice. Don't squeeze the bag; it may take a couple of hours. Place juice in refrigerator for about 8 hours.

Measure 8 cups juice. Place juice in lined colander over saucepan and strain. Add sugar to juice. Heat to 220°F.

Remove from heat, skim off foam, pour into jars, and leave ¼-inch headspace. Wipe rim, top with lids, and process.

Water-Bath Canner Processing Times for Half-Pints				
Altitude in Feet	0-1,000	1,001-3,000	3,001-6,000	6,001+
Processing Time	5 minutes	10 minutes	10 minutes	15 minutes

USING A JELLY BAG

Wet jelly bags before using. For a large batch of jelly, you need several bags—or lots of patience to strain batches.

If you don't have jelly bags, line a colander with 2 layers of dampened cheesecloth for the first and second straining.

Some people make a large jelly bag from thin cotton material, like an old T-shirt. Anything used will be stained permanently.

Don't squeeze the bags; this makes poor-quality juice and jelly. It can take several hours for each bag to drain.

REMOVING FOAM

Use large saucepans when cooking jelly, as the juice will foam and rise in the pan.

As the juice cooks, keep stirring to reduce the height of foam, and don't allow juice to boil over.

You can skim as the juice is cooking or wait until you remove it from the stove.

Special jelly skimmers are made to catch the foam, or foam will cling to a wooden or metal spoon. Work quickly so jelly doesn't start to firm up.

APPLE BUTTER

BEFORE PEANUT BUTTER BECAME POPULAR, ALMOST EVERY HOME HAD A STASH OF APPLE BUTTER

Every housewife used to have her own apple butter recipe—from dark and spicy to light and sweet. Apple butter is thicker and smoother than applesauce. The spices are more prominent in apple butter than in applesauce. This recipe is a moderately spicy one; you can adjust the spices to your family's preferences.

Apple butter is generally used as a condiment, smeared on bread or graham crackers for a quick snack. However, it can be used to make quick breads and muffins with a spicy apple taste. In Pennsylvanian Dutch cooking, apple and other fruit butters are usually used as sauces for meats. In some old recipes real butter is added to the fruit. *Yield: 8 pints*

What You Will Need

8 pounds apples

2 cups cider vinegar

2 cups apple cider or juice

Colander or food strainer

2¼ cups white sugar

2¼ cups brown sugar

2 tablespoons cinnamon

1 tablespoon ground cloves

1 tablespoon allspice

8 sterilized pint jars and lids

Water-bath canner

APPLE BUTTER

Wash, peel, core, and cut up apples. Combine apples, vinegar, and cider or juice in a saucepan. Simmer until soft, about 15 minutes.

Place soft apples in a food strainer or push through a colander. Return strained apples to saucepan along with sugars and spices.

Cook on low heat 4-5 hours and stir often. To test for doneness, place a spoonful on a plate. If liquid doesn't separate out at the edges, it is done. Remove from heat.

Pour apple butter into sterilized jars. Wipe rims, top with lids, and process.

Water-Bath Canner Processing Times for Pints				
Altitude in Feet	0-1,000	1,001-3,000	3,001-6,000	6,001+
Processing Time	5 minutes	10 minutes	10 minutes	15 minutes

Recipe Variations

Pear Butter: Use about 8 pounds peeled, cored pears in place of apples. Allow pears to ripen on the counter until soft before using them.

Peach Butter: Use about 10 pounds peaches in place of the apples. Peel peaches by dipping in boiling water and then cold, and then slipping off the skin. Remove pits.

COOKING THE APPLE BUTTER

Apple butter takes a long time to cook down to the right spreading consistency. It must be watched carefully during this time.

This is the one place in canning where a slow cooker might work to cook down the apples.

During cooking, the sugar caramelizes and adds to the flavor. Don't let it burn, however, because that flavor isn't appealing.

Enlist the help of friends or older children and make stirring the butter a shared ritual.

KNOWING WHEN IT'S DONE

After hours of cooking, the apple butter should look thick and slightly shiny.

Scoop out a big spoonful and place it on a plate. Let it cool a few minutes.

If it stays mounded in the center and no fluid seeps out to make a ring around it, it's done.

If fluid leaks from the apple butter, it needs to be cooked a little longer.

PEACH PRESERVES

THE WARMTH OF THE SUN IS CAPTURED IN LUSCIOUS PEACH PRESERVES

These sunny Peach Preserves will bring warmth to the coldest winter days. They are a sweet treat on toast or spooned over vanilla ice cream. They are also excellent smoothed over pound cake.

This is a very simple recipe and a good place to begin your jelly-, jam-, and preserve-making experience. It's a quick way to use a small surplus of peaches.

Choose ripe, juicy peaches. If they don't seem ripe enough, let them sit on the counter covered with dish towels for a few days.

Never use moldy peaches in canning, and cut out all brown, rotted spots. Overripe peaches do not make good preserves. *Yield: 7 half-pint jars*

What You Will Need

2 quarts peaches

6 cups sugar

7 sterilized half-pint jars and lids

Water-bath canner

PEACH PRESERVES

Wash and peel peaches. Remove pits and slice.

Layer peaches and sugar in a bowl. Place in refrigerator for 12 hours.

Transfer peach-sugar mixture to a saucepan. Heat to boiling and gently boil until mix thickens and becomes clear, about 45 minutes. Stir frequently.

Pour into hot, sterile jars, leave ¼-inch headspace. Wipe rims, top with lids, and process.

Water-Bath Canner Processing Times for Half-Pints				
Altitude in Feet	0-1,000	1,001-3,000	3,001-6,000	6,001+
Processing Time	5 minutes	10 minutes	10 minutes	15 minutes

Types of Preserves

Jelly is made from strained fruit juices and is thick but nearly clear. **Jam** contains pureed fruit and sometimes seeds. It has a uniform consistency that is thick enough to spread. **Preserves** have larger, identifiable pieces of fruit and are softer than jam. **Conserves** are like preserves but they have things like nuts and coconut added. **Marmalades** are like jelly that has fruit pieces folded into it.

BRINGING OUT THE JUICE

Sugar draws the fluid out of fruits. The peaches are layered with sugar and allowed to sit overnight.

Keep the peaches and sugar in the refrigerator to keep insects out of the mix. Cover the bowl to avoid picking up any flavor from other foods.

The sugar will partially dissolve in the peach juice.

There will be enough fluid to keep the sugar from scorching in the pan as cooking begins.

COOKING THE PEACHES

Peaches have enough pectin and acid that when combined with the right amount of sugar will generally make a nice gel.

Cook the mixture slowly; keep it at a gentle boil. Stir frequently to keep the mixture from scorching.

Preserves do not get as thick as jam. The mixture should look thick and shiny when finished, but will pour off a spoon when warm.

If foam develops, quickly skim it off just before pouring preserves into jars.

BACON & TOMATO JAM
THIS ODD-SOUNDING JAM IS DELICIOUS ON TOAST

This is actually an older recipe that has had a recent surge in popularity. It's different and intriguing and a good way to use up a few extra ripe tomatoes.

Try it on toast or mixed with scrambled eggs. A piece of smoked turkey on a nice roll with this jam is also tasty.

A big platter of home-fried potatoes served with Bacon & Tomato Jam slathered over them is a mouthwatering treat and a great way to present this jam.

You can add spices such as red pepper or garlic, if you like. The salt could be left out. Sugar is necessary to get the thick texture, and artificial sweeteners will not work as substitutes. *Yield: 4 half-pint jars*

What You Will Need

1 pound bacon

4 pounds ripe tomatoes

2 medium onions

2 cups sugar

⅓ cup cider vinegar

1 tablespoon salt

½ teaspoon black pepper

4 half-pint freezer containers or freezer-safe glass jars and lids

BACON AND TOMATO JAM

Fry bacon until crisp; drain off grease. Break into small pieces.

Wash tomatoes, remove core, and chop into small pieces. Peel onions and mince into small pieces.

Place tomatoes, onions, sugar, vinegar, and spices in saucepan. Bring to a boil. Add bacon pieces.

Cook at a simmer, stirring frequently, until mixture is very thick, about 1 hour. Pour into clean freezer containers and cool. Freeze all jam that will not be eaten within 4 days. Keep unfrozen jam in refrigerator.

PREPARING THE BACON

PREPARING TOMATOES AND ONIONS

Use your favorite brand of bacon or use bacon ends and pieces to save money.

Cook the bacon with a bacon press or weigh it down so it cooks evenly and completely. It should be cooked until crisp.

Drain the bacon on paper towels and crunch it up into small pieces.

You can also purchase real bacon bits or precooked bacon to use in this recipe.

You do not need to peel the tomatoes in this recipe, although you can do so if you like.

Dice the tomatoes into small pieces and mince the onion as finely as possible.

Stir the mixture often as it cooks. In the last few minutes, as the moisture cooks off, stir continuously.

The jam is done when it is thick and glossy and mounds on a spoon.

ORANGE MARMALADE

SWEET, YET TANGY, THIS OLD-TIME FAVORITE MAKES AN EXCELLENT GIFT

Orange marmalade speaks of English high tea and a plate of scones. You either like it or you don't. If you do, you may want to use this recipe to make fresh homemade marmalade—it's an excellent way to preserve excess backyard oranges.

This recipe makes a pretty gift, especially with a plate of scones or tea cookies. It also serves as an excellent company dessert when spread over orange pound cake.

Orange marmalade is sometimes used in cooking, especially with poultry like duck or goose.

Tangerines can be used for some of the oranges, and limes can be used in place of the lemons. *Yield: 7 half-pint jars*

What You Will Need

6 large oranges

2 medium lemons

6 cups water

6 cups white sugar

Jelly or candy thermometer

7 half-pint sterilized jars and lids

Water-bath canner

ORANGE MARMALADE

Separate the peel from the oranges and lemons and save. Chop the peeled fruit and remove the seeds.

Take saved peels and slice into thin strips. Place peel, fruit, and water in saucepan and simmer 5 minutes. Remove mixture from heat and refrigerate for 12 hours.

Add sugar to mixture and heat slowly, stirring to dissolve sugar. Then briskly boil, stirring occasionally, until temperature reads 220°F, about 30 minutes.

Pour marmalade into jars, leave ¼-inch headspace. Wipe rim, top with lids, and process.

Water-Bath Canner Processing Times for Half-Pints				
Altitude in Feet	0-1,000	1,001-3,000	3,001-6,000	6,001+
Processing Time	5 minutes	10 minutes	10 minutes	15 minutes

PREPARING THE PEELS

The peel contributes to the flavor and texture of the marmalade, giving it a bitter taste.

The white membrane under the peel contains pectin, which causes the marmalade to gel.

Wash the skin of the oranges and lemons carefully in hot water before peeling and remove any wax or coatings.

Use a sharp knife and slice the peel into very tiny pieces. The peel can also be coarsely grated.

COOKING THE MARMALADE

The first cooking breaks down enzymes and allows oils from the peels to seep out to flavor the mix.

The peels will soften during the resting period, and flavors will intensify.

When you add the sugar and bring the mixture to a boil, use a jelly thermometer for best results.

At 220°F the mixture will be thick and shiny and will cling to a spoon held over the pot, dripping off very slowly. Do not overcook.

APPLE JUICE

MAKE YOUR OWN APPLE JUICE FOR DRINKING OR COOKING

A lot of the apple juice sold in grocery stores comes from other countries. It can contain preservatives, sugar, or corn syrup. You can make your own family- and earth-friendly apple juice quite easily at home.

Apple juice used to be the drink of choice for families, before soda and before refrigerators were invented to keep milk cool. Some preferred to let their apple juice sit and ferment, making hard cider,

the early equivalent of bottled beer. Your apple juice will remain nonalcoholic if you can it.

You can use less-than-perfect apples for juice, but do avoid molded and mushy, overly ripe apples. Each batch of apple juice usually has its own unique flavor, just like fine wines. *Yield: About 1 quart per 3 pounds apples*

What You Will Need

3 pounds apples per quart of juice (several varieties mixed make the best juice)

1 cup water for every pound of apples

Fruit press or strainer or food processor

Jelly bag and stand or colander lined with 2 layers cheesecloth

About ½ cup sugar per quart of juice (optional)

Sterilized quart jars and lids

Water-bath canner

APPLE JUICE

Wash apples. Slice off each end; discard. Do not core or peel. Cut apples into chunks.

For every 3 cups of chunked apples, add 1 cup water to a large pot. Cover and simmer for about 25 minutes, until apples are soft. Drain.

Mash or puree apples. Pour into jelly bag or colander lined with cheesecloth; collect juice.

Place juice in saucepan; add sugar if desired. Heat to boiling. Pour into jars, wipe rims, top with lids, and process.

Water-Bath Canner Processing Times for Quarts				
Altitude in Feet	0-1,000	1,001-3,000	3,001-6,000	6,001+
Processing Time	5 minutes	10 minutes	10 minutes	15 minutes

MAKE IT EASY

If you don't grow apples, you may want to save time and contact a cider mill that uses local apples. Ask to buy freshly pressed juice (cider) and then strain it and process it for canning. Even if it's pasteurized at the mill, the strained juice needs to be canned for long-term storage. Fresh cider can be frozen, then strained and processed later.

CHOOSING APPLES FOR JUICE

A mixture of tart and sweet apples makes the best juice. Apples vary in sweetness by variety and by subtle differences in climate and weather each year.

Apples require two different varieties to set fruit, so even homeowners may have different apple varieties. If you don't, consider swapping with a neighbor.

Small, odd-shaped, scabby, and lightly bruised apples are no problem for juice making.

You'll want to avoid wormy, moldy, heavily damaged, or frozen apples.

MASHING THE APPLES

Some large commercial mills cold press apples, but you will get more juice by heating them.

You can put the cooked apples through a food processor if you are careful not to lose juice, the desired product.

Mash the apple pulp well—you can use a hand mixer or potato masher.

Straining removes skin, seeds, and pulp and leaves you with amber, clear juice. Straining can take several hours. Don't squeeze or push pulp through the strainer for clear juice.

GRAPE JUICE

AN OLD-TIME FAVORITE WITH LOTS OF HEALTH BENEFITS

No mashing grapes with your feet here. Our grape juice–making recipe is a little more hygienic. Your canned grape juice won't turn into wine on you, unless you want it to—but that's another book.

Even one prolific grapevine can leave you with more grapes than you can use fresh, and making juice is a good way to use them.

Concord grapes, developed from wild North American grapes, are the premier grape for juice making. But you can make grape juice from any grapes, including wild ones. The color of the juice will reflect the grape color. Like apples, the sweetness of grapes varies by the variety and growing conditions; you'll want to adjust the sweetness to your taste. *Yield: 7 quarts*

What You Will Need

25 pounds grapes (a mix of varieties is fine)

Boiling water

Jelly bag or colander lined with 2 layers cheesecloth

Strainer lined with a coffee filter

2 cups sugar, or to taste (optional)

7 sterilized quart jars with lids

Water-bath canner

GRAPE JUICE

Wash grapes and put into a large pot. Pour in just enough boiling water to cover grapes.

Cook on simmer until skins are soft. Pour grapes with fluid into jelly bag or lined colander. Collect juice.

Place in refrigerator for 12 hours. Carefully remove juice from the top, leaving sediment layer. Return juice to pot, pouring through lined strainer.

Heat to boiling, add sugar, stir to dissolve, and remove. Pour into hot jars, leaving ¼-inch headspace. Wipe rim, top with lids, process.

Water-Bath Canner Processing Times for Quarts				
Altitude in Feet	0-1,000	1,001-3,000	3,001-6,000	6,001+
Processing Time	5 minutes	10 minutes	10 minutes	15 minutes

Grape Tips

Concord grapes are the top juice grape, but there are other varieties that will work. Catawba, Delaware, and Canadice are good dark-colored grapes for home juice production. Niagara and Himrod are good white juice choices. Wild grapes can be used but require extra sweetening. Mixing two varieties can improve flavor.

DECANTING THE JUICE

When grape juice sits, particularly when it's chilled, chemicals in it form tartrate crystals. These are harmless, but some people dislike the look and feel of them.

Tartrate crystals can be clear or colored like the juice and look like shards of glass.

Small pieces of pulp and other things will also settle to the bottom, forming a sediment layer.

The top grape juice should be ladled off or carefully poured off and the sediment layer discarded.

DOUBLE STRAINING THE JUICE

After the sediment is discarded, the juice should be strained again. Pouring it through coffee filters will leave a very clean juice.

Two layers of damp cheesecloth in a colander will also work. Double straining takes time but results in a top-quality product.

When working with grape juice, be very careful, as it will stain anything it touches.

Once the juice has been strained, you need to heat it to boiling before you pour it into jars.

APRICOT NECTAR

SWEET, SMOOTH, AND DELICIOUS, APRICOT NECTAR IS GOOD FROM SIPPY CUP TO COCKTAIL GLASS

Apricot nectar is almost a guilty pleasure; it's addicting, truly a drink of the gods. In earlier days it was brought to the table with a carafe of ice water and mixed with water to each person's taste.

This juice is also a delightful mixer for alcoholic beverages. Apricot-nectar punches are for those with exquisite taste. Nectar is also used for baking and as a meat glaze.

Apricot nectar is really thick, sweetened apricot juice. Peaches, papaya, and pears are also used in nectars. These thick juices are sometimes called "honey."

What You Will Need

16 cups chopped, pitted apricots
(about a peck fresh)

4 cups water

Food strainer or fine sieve

1½ cups white sugar

¼ cup lemon juice

¼ teaspoon nutmeg

9 sterilized pint jars and lids

Water-bath canner

APRICOT NECTAR

Wash apricots, remove pits, and chop. Measure 16 cups.

Bring water to a boil in a large pot and add apricots. Simmer about 5 minutes or until fruit is soft.

Place soft apricots in food strainer or push through fine sieve. Place the thick fluid in a pot with sugar, lemon juice, and nutmeg. Bring just to a boil, stirring constantly. Remove from heat.

Pour nectar into jars, wipe rims, top with lids, and process.

Apricot nectar is sold at high prices in stores, but it's simple and easy to make your own. *Yield: 9 pints*

Water-Bath Canner Processing Times for Pints				
Altitude in Feet	0-1,000	1,001-3,000	3,001-6,000	6,001+
Processing Time	15 minutes	20 minutes	20 minutes	25 minutes

Important

This recipe uses pint jars because the juice is very thick. Thicker products take longer to heat to a safe bacteria-killing level. Processing times are for pint jars only. In canning recipes, never substitute different-size jars unless the recipe mentions it. Since most people use small amounts at a time, the pint jar is a convenient size. A pint jar equals 2 cups apricot nectar.

SIEVING THE PULP

In this recipe it isn't necessary to peel the apricots. Just wash them well and remove the pits.

Apricots soften quickly. After the water comes to a boil, turn it down and just let the fruit simmer softly.

Push the apricots through a food sieve or mash them by hand through a fine strainer.

In this case it is fine to use force to get as much juice as you can.

USING APRICOT NECTAR

Cake: Use nectar in place of water in a yellow or white cake mix.

Apricot Tea: Combine 2½ cups nectar, 1 cup orange juice, 1 cup water, 2 teaspoons instant tea, and sugar to taste.

Apricot Dessert: Dissolve 6-ounce box orange gelatin in 2 cups boiling water. Add 2 cups nectar and 1 6-ounce can crushed pineapple. Chill until firm.

Apricot Glaze: Combine 1 cup nectar, ½ cup honey, and 2 teaspoons dry mustard. Spread on meat.

CRANBERRY JUICE

THIS POPULAR HEALTH JUICE IS EASY TO MAKE

Along with grape juice, cranberry juice has some great health benefits associated with it. It's high in antioxidants and contains chemicals that make it hard for bacteria to cling to the urinary tract, so it is often used to help bladder infections.

While it isn't as easy to make as some juices, you can make cranberry juice at home. If you are in a cranberry-growing region and can find berries locally, your juice will probably cost less than commercial juice.

Cranberry juice is tart, and other fruit juices are frequently blended with it. You can do that too, or sweeten the juice to your taste with sugar. Apple and cherry juice are good for blending with cranberry juice. *Yield: 1 quart per 5 pounds berries*

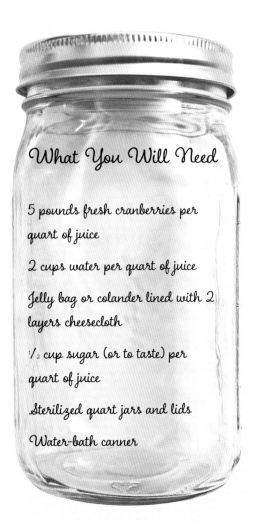

What You Will Need

5 pounds fresh cranberries per quart of juice

2 cups water per quart of juice

Jelly bag or colander lined with 2 layers cheesecloth

½ cup sugar (or to taste) per quart of juice

Sterilized quart jars and lids

Water-bath canner

CRANBERRY JUICE

Wash cranberries. Discard green or soft berries. Place in pot with just enough water to cover. Simmer cranberries 5 minutes, or until most cranberries have split skins. Do not boil.

Pour mixture into jelly bag or colander; collect juice. Return pulp to pan, add water to barely cover, simmer 5 minutes. Pour mixture through jelly bag or colander; collect juice.

Heat all juice just to a boil, turn off heat, and stir in sugar until dissolved. Pour into jars, leaving ½-inch headspace. Wipe rims, top with lids, and process.

Water-Bath Canner Processing Times for Quarts				
Altitude in Feet	0-1,000	1,001-3,000	3,001-6,000	6,001+
Processing Time	5 minutes	10 minutes	10 minutes	15 minutes

Recipe Variation

Cherry Juice: Tart cherry juice is extremely expensive in stores. The benefits of tart cherry juice are almost as legendary as cranberry juice. You can use this recipe to make tart cherry juice if cherries are more abundant in your region. Be sure to pit cherries before making juice. It takes about 2 quarts of cherries to make a quart of juice. Sweet cherries can also be used for juice.

SECOND JUICE COLLECTION

Cranberries are firm and don't yield juice easily.

Heat is required to soften the berries. When they have split skins and feel soft, mash them with a potato masher or big spoon in the cooking water.

Pour smashed berries and juice into the jelly bag and save the juice that drips through.

Return the pulp from the jelly bag to the pot and heat for a second time. Then refill the jelly bag and allow additional juice to drip through.

SWEETEN TO TASTE

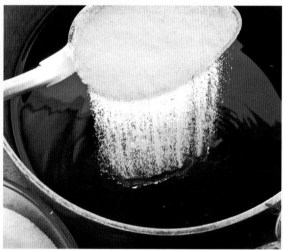

For each quart of juice, ½ cup sugar will make mildly sweet juice. You may want to add up to 1 more cup of sugar.

For low-sugar juice add no sugar. Remember that fruit has natural sugars. When you are ready to use the juice, you can add artificial sweeteners to taste.

Cranberry juice can be mixed with apple, grape, orange, or berry juices for unique blends.

Bring all juices to a boil before filling jars.

TOMATO JUICE

GREAT FOR DRINKING, COOKING, OR MIXING YOUR FAVORITE DRINK

Many people enjoy a daily glass of tomato juice. It's full of vitamins and healthful flavonoids. Tomato juice is extremely versatile in the kitchen, forming a base for soups and sauces. It also tenderizes meat when meat is slow cooked or marinated in it.

The salt in this recipe is not necessary for safe canning and can be left out. You must, however, add the lemon juice to each jar to acidify the juice and make it safe to can in a water-bath canner. Choose really ripe slicing tomatoes rather than paste type for the most juice. Tomatoes of any color can be made into juice, but yellow tomato juice, for example, may not be as visually appealing. *Yield: 7 quarts*

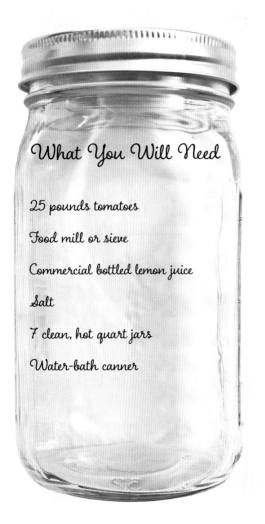

What You Will Need

25 pounds tomatoes

Food mill or sieve

Commercial bottled lemon juice

Salt

7 clean, hot quart jars

Water-bath canner

TOMATO JUICE

Wash tomatoes; cut out bad spots, but do not peel. Crush 5 tomatoes in a large pot. Bring to a boil.

Keep tomatoes boiling; slice the rest of the tomatoes and add. Boil 5 minutes when finished.

Put tomatoes through food mill or push through sieve. Discard skins and seeds. Put juice in pot; boil 1 minute.

Add 2 tablespoons lemon juice and 1 teaspoon salt to each jar. Pour juice into jars, leaving ½-inch headspace. Wipe rims, top with lids, and process.

Water-Bath Canner Processing Times for Quarts				
Altitude in Feet	0-1,000	1,001-3,000	3,001-6,000	6,001+
Processing Time	40 minutes	45 minutes	50 minutes	55 minutes

Tomato Juice Uses

There are dozens of ways to use tomato juice. With added spices, use it to marinate meat overnight. Use as a base for soup or stew. If you're a vegetarian, use tomato juice in place of broth in many recipes. You can also slow cook tough meat in it or cook pasta, beans, or rice in it instead of water. Mix with beer for a popular Canadian or Mexican drink (or use the mix to baste grilling meat).

ADDING TOMATOES TO POT

When your first tomatoes are boiling, adding more to the pot must be done carefully so the hot juice doesn't splatter and cause a mess or burns.

Fill a small bowl with sliced tomatoes and get it close to the boiling liquid before you gently slide the contents into the pot.

Tomato juice will stain clothing, so wear an apron or old clothes when canning juice.

Watch the juice and stir occasionally while it's cooking. It's thick and can scorch.

ACIDIFYING THE JUICE

Tomatoes vary in the amount of acidity they have. To be safe, all tomato products should have added acid.

Carefully measure 2 tablespoons lemon juice into each jar before you fill them. You add the salt now, too, if you're using it.

The lemon juice must be commercially bottled, concentrated, real lemon juice, not home-squeezed juice or lemon-flavored juice.

Commercial 5 percent vinegar can be substituted for the lemon juice but will give the juice a stronger flavor.

MIXED VEGETABLE JUICE

THIS HEALTHY DRINK USES UP SURPLUS GARDEN VEGGIES

You could use a juicer and make fresh vegetable juice each time you want it. But let's face it: Most of us would rather open a jar. Make a lot of juice at one time when vegetables are fresh, local, and abundant, and can it for convenient use later.

You can use vegetable juice in soups and stews and as a cooking liquid. When you make your own, you can vary the spices to suit your taste. You can also vary the ingredients, but the ratio must remain 22 pounds of tomatoes to 3 cups of other vegetables.

You can leave out the salt in this recipe, but remember to add the lemon juice so the mix is acidic enough to can safely. *Yield: 7 quarts*

What You Will Need

22 pounds ripe tomatoes

1 cup thinly sliced unpeeled carrots

1 cup chopped onion

1 cup thinly sliced celery

Food strainer or sieve

3 tablespoons salt (optional)

7 clean, hot quart jars with lids

Commercially bottled lemon juice

Water-bath canner

MIXED VEGETABLE JUICE

Wash tomatoes and cut off stem end.

Crush tomatoes in a pot; add remaining vegetables. Bring to a boil, turn down heat, and simmer 20 minutes.

Pour vegetables into strainer or mash through sieve to collect juice. Discard seeds and skins.

Return juice to pot, add salt, and bring to a boil. Pour into jars. Add 2 tablespoons lemon juice to each jar, wipe rims, top with lids, and process.

Water-Bath Canner Processing Times for Quarts				
Altitude in Feet	0-1,000	1,001-3,000	3,001-6,000	6,001+
Processing Time	40 minutes	45 minutes	50 minutes	55 minutes

Recipe Variation

Choose a combined total of 3 cups of any of these vegetables to add to 22 pounds of tomatoes: peppers (hot or sweet), celery, cabbage, onions, carrots, turnips, beets. Wash the vegetables and slice or chop them before measuring. Only onions need to be peeled. You can also add chopped firm fruit, such as apples.

ONLY THREE CUPS

Because most vegetables are not acidic, tomatoes are used as the base for mixed vegetable juices.

If you stay within 3 cups added nonacidic vegetables to 22 pounds tomatoes, the mixture can be water-bath canned.

Three cups of most vegetables will be enough to flavor the juice. Three cups of onions would probably be too strong tasting.

You can use 4 tablespoons vinegar or ½ teaspoon citric acid per quart instead of lemon juice.

SALT IS OPTIONAL

For salt-free diets it's safe to leave the salt out of this recipe.

Don't use salt substitutes in this recipe. They can leave off flavors or cause discoloration or sediment in the juice.

Other spices are safe to use. Try garlic powder, black pepper, paprika, cayenne pepper, cumin, and/or chili powder.

Leafy herbs such as cilantro, parsley, celery leaf, and oregano could be cooked with the vegetables if they are strained out before canning.

WHOLE TOMATOES

TOMATOES ARE ALMOST INDISPENSABLE IN THE KITCHEN

Tomatoes are often one of the first things people attempt to can. They're a good thing to start with because they are fairly easy to can in a variety of ways.

Most gardeners grow tomatoes and often have more than they can eat fresh. They are found at farmers' markets everywhere should you need to buy them.

You can consider yourself quite "green" if you can local tomatoes in season to use in the winter instead of buying hard, tasteless tomatoes shipped thousands of miles.

If you are going to grow tomatoes primarily for canning, choose "determinate" types of tomatoes. This means they will ripen their crop close together, instead of spreading the ripening over a long season. *Yield: 7 quarts*

What You Will Need

85–90 medium tomatoes

Water, about 10 cups

Colander or strainer

1 cup commercially bottled lemon juice

2½ tablespoons salt (canning salt works best)

7 clean, hot quart jars and lids

Water-bath canner

WHOLE TOMATOES

Wash and peel tomatoes.

Core tomatoes, and put them in a large pot. Cover with water and boil gently for 5 minutes.

Add 2 tablespoons lemon juice and ½ teaspoon salt to each jar. Spoon whole tomatoes (or cut in half) into jars. Ladle hot cooking water over them, leaving ½-inch headspace.

Remove bubbles, wipe rims, top with lids, and process.

Water-Bath Canner Processing Times for Quarts				
Altitude in Feet	0-1,000	1,001-3,000	3,001-6,000	6,001+
Processing Time	45 minutes	50 minutes	55 minutes	60 minutes

Tomato Tips

Tomatoes come in literally thousands of varieties. There are many colors, sizes, and flavors. All tomatoes can be canned, but some are better than others for canning. Good paste-type tomatoes include Roma, Opalka, San Marzano, Sausage, and Amish Paste. Determinate tomatoes for high canning yields include Legend, Wisconsin 55, Heinz 1439, Mountain Fresh, Campbell 33, Homestead, Marglobe, Rutgers PS, and Oregon Spring.

PEELING TOMATOES

Tomatoes are blanched to peel them. You need a pot of boiling water and a pot of ice water.

Using a colander or strainer, lower several tomatoes into the boiling water.

Count to 60 slowly and then quickly place the colander in the ice water for 60 seconds.

The skins of the tomatoes should split and peel. The tomatoes may still be hot, so you may want to use gloves to pull off the skins.

FILLING JARS

The lemon juice and salt are measured and put in the bottom of each jar. Processing will distribute them through the jar later.

Use a slotted spoon to lift tomatoes. Pack jars solidly without crushing the tomatoes.

Ladle the cooking water over the tomatoes in the jars. Use a bubble stick, then add more fluid if needed.

If you run short of cooking water, bring some additional water to a boil and use that to cover tomatoes.

CRUSHED TOMATOES

INVALUABLE IN MANY DISHES, ALWAYS KEEP A GOOD SUPPLY

Crushed tomatoes are the basis for many sauces and are very useful in the kitchen. They have seeds and some chunks of tomato and are a little less thick than tomato paste. They make an excellent base for chili and soup.

A smart cook keeps a variety of tomato products on hand to make various recipes quickly. The recipe below has little seasoning, but you can add additional seasoning such as garlic and oregano if you like. If you do add spices and herbs, add that information on the jar label.

Don't forget the lemon juice that goes into each jar so it's acidic enough to can safely. *Yield: 7 quarts*

What You Will Need

85–90 medium tomatoes

2½ tablespoons salt

2 teaspoons black pepper

¾ cup lemon juice

7 clean, hot quart jars and lids

Water-bath canner

CRUSHED TOMATOES

Place tomatoes in boiling water and then in cold water; slip off skins, remove core, and quarter.

Put 3 cups tomato quarters into a large pot and crush with a spoon while heating. Add salt and pepper.

Bring to a boil, stirring constantly. Gradually add remaining tomatoes, but do not crush. Cook, stirring constantly, 5 minutes.

Put 2 tablespoons lemon juice in each jar. Fill with tomatoes, leaving ½-inch headspace. Remove bubbles, wipe rims, place lids, and process.

Water-Bath Canner Processing Times for Quarts				
Altitude in Feet	0–1,000	1,001–3,000	3,001–6,000	6,001+
Processing Time	45 minutes	50 minutes	55 minutes	60 minutes

Easy Chili

Brown 1 pound ground beef with 1 medium onion, finely chopped, in a large pot. Drain off the grease. Add to the pot 1 quart crushed tomatoes and 1 12-ounce can kidney beans. Add 2 tablespoons chili powder or to taste. Cook at a simmer for about 30 minutes, stirring frequently. After filling bowls, sprinkle with finely shredded cheddar cheese. *Yield: 2 quarts*

MAKING JUICE

You crush the first few tomatoes to produce juice; this helps prevent juice from separating later.

The rest of the tomatoes will gradually break down during cooking and don't need to be crushed with a spoon.

Stir the tomatoes constantly, because the mixture will become quite thick as the tomatoes break down and it may scorch.

If you want to add spices, do so during the cooking period so they blend with the tomatoes.

ACIDIFYING THE JARS

Add 2 tablespoons commercially bottled concentrated lemon juice to each jar before you fill them with crushed tomatoes.

Four tablespoons vinegar or ½ teaspoon citric acid can be used instead of lemon juice. The vinegar may leave a flavor.

Pour the hot crushed tomatoes through a jar funnel slowly to cause fewer bubbles.

Never can a jar that is filled less than ½ inch from the rim. Smaller amounts should be refrigerated and used right away.

TOMATO PASTE
GOOD TOMATO PASTE IS A KITCHEN STAPLE

All tomatoes can be cooked down to paste, but starting with paste-type tomatoes, often called Roma tomatoes, will make a faster, smoother product. Juicy tomatoes may take twice as long to cook down. Paste tomatoes are often oblong, with thick flesh and less juice and gel inside.

As with other tomato products, tomato paste is the perfect start to many recipes. This is canned in small jars because it is thick and would need a lot of time to process in larger jars. It is also a convenient size for most recipes, because you often don't need much of it and opened store-bought cans can grow moldy if not used quickly. Do not change the jar size.

You can leave out the salt and adjust the spices to your taste. *Yield: 9 half-pint jars*

What You Will Need

About 100 paste-type tomatoes

1½ cups finely chopped sweet red peppers

1 teaspoon canning salt (optional)

½ teaspoon garlic powder (optional)

Sieve or food processor

9 clean, hot half-pint jars

Water-bath canner

TOMATO PASTE

Wash tomatoes. Place in boiling water and then in cold water; slip off skins, remove core, and chop.

Place all ingredients in a pot and simmer for 1 hour. Then push mixture through a sieve or blend in food processor until smooth.

Return to pot and simmer until thick, about 2 hours. Stir frequently.

Pour hot paste into jars, remove bubbles, wipe rims, top with lids, and process.

Water-Bath Canner Processing Times for Half-Pints			
Altitude in Feet	0–1,000	1,001–3,000	3,001–6,000	6,001+
Processing Time	45 minutes	50 minutes	55 minutes	60 minutes

IS IT THICK ENOUGH?

Tomato paste takes a long time to cook down, especially if you start with regular tomatoes.

Don't cover the cooking pot—you want the steam to escape.

As the mixture gets thicker, it will require more frequent stirring to keep it from scorching.

When paste is done, it will have been reduced to about half the original volume. It will mound on a spoon without running off.

REMOVING BUBBLES

Air bubbles rise to the surface during processing and leave a large space at the top of the jar.

After pouring hot paste into the jars, run a bubble stick slowly back and forth through the jar and around the sides.

This releases trapped air and settles the contents. Fill with additional paste if needed.

Any thin plastic or wooden item can be used if you don't have a bubble stick. Don't use metal objects; they may damage the jars.

ITALIAN TOMATO SAUCE
GREAT FOR PASTA, PIZZA, AND SO MUCH MORE!

This is a wonderful cooking sauce you'll enjoy using for all kinds of Italian cooking. You will notice it has a lot of ingredients, and because of this, it cannot be safely processed in a water-bath canner. If you don't have a pressure canner, you can make this and freeze it.

There is a lot of food prep in this recipe, so it's good to save this activity for a rainy day when you have lots of time to work.

You can modify the spices to suit your taste. The kitchen will smell wonderful while this is cooking, and you may want to have your favorite pizza crust baking so you can taste the sauce right away. *Yield: 7 quarts*

What You Will Need

30 pounds tomatoes; paste types work best

Sieve or food strainer

1/4 cup olive oil

1 cup chopped onions

1 cup chopped green peppers

1 pound fresh mushrooms, sliced

1/4 cup brown sugar

1/2 teaspoon garlic powder

2 teaspoons black pepper

4 1/2 teaspoons canning salt

4 tablespoons minced fresh oregano

4 tablespoons minced fresh basil

7 clean, hot quart jars and lids

Pressure canner

ITALIAN TOMATO SAUCE

Blanch, peel, and chop tomatoes. Place in a pot and boil 20 minutes. Put through sieve or food strainer; return to pot.

Heat oil in a frying pan; cook onions, green peppers, and mushrooms until soft. Add to tomatoes.

Add sugar and seasonings except oregano and basil. Bring to a boil, reduce to simmer, stirring frequently, for 45 minutes. Add herbs and simmer until thick.

Pour sauce into jars, leaving 1-inch headspace. Remove bubbles, wipe rims, place lids, and process.

Pressure Canner Processing of Quarts for 25 minutes				
Altitude in Feet	0-2,000	2,001-4,000	4,001-6,000	6,001+
Dial Gauge	11 pounds	12 pounds	13 pounds	14 pounds
Altitude in Feet	0-1,000	1,001+		

Recipe Variation

Mexican Sauce: Replace the green peppers and mushrooms in the Italian sauce recipe with 2 cups hot peppers (chiles, serrano, and so on), finely chopped, seeds and white membrane removed. Replace the basil with 4 tablespoons minced cilantro and replace black pepper with 1 tablespoon ground cumin. Proceed with recipe. Use on tacos and in spicy dips.

COOKING THE VEGETABLES

Make sure to finely chop the onions and peppers and thinly slice the mushrooms.

Pour the olive oil (or substitute vegetable oil) into a frying pan and heat until sizzling.

Add onions, peppers, and mushrooms. Cook and stir until onions are clear and peppers are soft.

Add vegetables to tomatoes and cook until the sauce is thick and smooth. Some pieces of vegetables will be visible. Stir frequently to prevent scorching.

ADDING THE HERBS

Wash the herbs and pat them dry. Remove thick stems.

Place the herbs on a cutting board and mince them finely with a sharp knife. Measure 4 tablespoons of each.

You can also use a food processor or kitchen shears to mince the herbs.

Add the herbs in the last 30 minutes of cooking for the best flavor. Large pieces can be strained out before jars are filled.

DICED WITH ONIONS & PEPPERS

USE THESE CANNED TOMATOES IN PLACE OF FRESH ON SALADS OR IN SOUPS AND CHILI

One problem with eating locally and seasonally is that you probably won't have fresh tomatoes for salads and sandwiches year-round. It takes a little getting used to, but canned, diced tomatoes can replace those hard, tasteless, out-of-season tomatoes for those uses. They are a little softer, but the taste is real garden tomato.

When you replace out-of-season tomatoes with your canned tomatoes, you'll get better flavor and nutrition and have the satisfaction of knowing you did a "green" thing.

What You Will Need

5–6 pounds tomatoes

½ cup chopped onions

½ cup chopped green peppers

1½ tablespoons celery salt

1 tablespoon sugar

6 clean, hot pint jars and lids

Pressure canner

DICED WITH ONIONS AND PEPPERS

Wash and core tomatoes, but do not peel. Cut into small chunks; measure 16 cups.

Combine all ingredients in a large saucepan. Bring to a boil.

Reduce heat, cover, and cook 5 minutes, stirring frequently.

Pour mix into hot jars, leaving ½-inch headspace. Remove bubbles, wipe rims, place lids, and process.

Diced tomatoes can be used in soups, casseroles, pasta dishes, and even omelets. They can also be a simple side dish for any meal. *Yield: 6 pints*

Pressure Canner Processing of Pints for 15 minutes				
Altitude in Feet	0-2,000	2,001-4,000	4,001-6,000	6,001+
Dial Gauge	11 pounds	12 pounds	13 pounds	14 pounds
Altitude in Feet	0-1,000	1,001+		

MAKE IT EASY

To use canned diced tomatoes on a salad, drain off the juice, reserving a tablespoon or two, and toss the tomatoes with 2 tablespoons olive or vegetable oil and the reserved juice. Place on the salad. You can use this as the sole dressing on the salad—it's low calorie! Add garlic and pepper or other spices. You can add your favorite salad dressing to the salad as well.

DICING THE TOMATOES

You can peel the tomatoes, but the peel won't bother you any more than it does on fresh tomatoes.

Slice tomatoes in half and remove the thicker core area on the stem end. Try to scrape out most of the seeds, but don't worry if a few slip through.

Cut the halves in two and in two again if the tomato is large. Don't make the pieces too small; you want to recognize them after cooking.

Save all the juice you can when cutting the tomatoes and add it to the pot.

DON'T OVERCOOK

While you want the peppers and onions to be soft, you don't want to cook the tomatoes until they are mush.

Stir gently and avoid crushing tomatoes. You want something closer to whole tomatoes in juice rather than sauce.

Put the pieces in jars with a slotted spoon. Then fill with cooking fluid.

Because this recipe uses onions and peppers, a pressure canner is needed to safely can the tomatoes.

BASIC TOMATO SALSA

START WITH THIS SIMPLE RECIPE AND INVENT YOUR OWN ZESTY TWISTS

Salsa was essentially unknown in the United States 50 years ago, but it's a big favorite now. Everyone has his or her idea of what salsa should look and taste like; this recipe is relatively mild and simple, but it can be modified in several ways.

Paste-type tomatoes are recommended for salsa making, but any tomatoes can be used. Juicier tomatoes will make a somewhat thinner salsa.

Salsa is great with chips, added to pasta for a quick salad, as a topper for steak or burgers, and of course on tacos, enchiladas, and burritos. This recipe can also be used without canning, but refrigerate until used and use within 3 to 4 days. *Yield: 8 pints*

What You Will Need

- 5 pounds paste-type Roma tomatoes
- 2½ cups chopped onions
- 1 tablespoon chopped fresh cilantro (optional)
- Plastic or rubber gloves
- 2 cups chopped fresh green chiles
- ¼ cup chopped jalapeño pepper
- ½ teaspoon garlic powder
- 1 tablespoon salt
- ½ tablespoon black pepper
- 1 tablespoon ground cumin (optional)
- 1½ tablespoons dried oregano (optional)
- 1 cup bottled lime juice
- 8 clean, hot pint jars with lids
- Water-bath canner

BASIC TOMATO SALSA

Dip tomatoes in boiling water, then cold. Remove the skins and chop. Measure 14 cups.

Combine tomatoes, onions, cilantro (if using), chiles, and jalapeño in a large pot over high heat.

Bring mixture to a boil, reduce heat, and simmer 10 minutes, stirring frequently. Add herbs, seasonings, and lime juice; simmer 20 minutes.

Pour salsa into jars, leaving ½-inch headspace. Remove bubbles, wipe rims, place lids, and process.

Water-Bath Canner Processing Times for Pints				
Altitude in Feet	0-1,000	1,001-3,000	3,001-6,000	6,001+
Processing Time	15 minutes	20 minutes	20 minutes	25 minutes

Recipe Variation

Don't increase the amount of onions; they can be left out altogether. Tomatillos, husked and chopped, can be used in place of some or all of the onion. Green peppers or yellow wax peppers can be substituted for all or part of the chiles for milder salsa. Any hot pepper can be substituted as well. Keep the proportion of peppers to tomatoes the same. Spices and salt can be altered.

CLEANING HOT PEPPERS

MEASURE CAREFULLY

Use gloves and keep your hands away from your face when chopping hot peppers. They can cause painful burns.

Cut off the stem end and tip and then split the pepper in half with a sharp knife.

The white membrane that holds the seeds is where a great deal of the pepper's "heat" comes from.

Scrape out the seeds and remove most of the white membrane with your thumb or a spoon. Doing this under running water is helpful.

Salsa recipes combine acidic tomatoes with nonacidic ingredients, and the proportions should not be altered for safe water-bath canning.

Measure the ingredients after they are cleaned and chopped. Don't assume a certain amount of fresh produce will produce the required recipe amount.

If you substitute hotter or milder peppers, do so carefully, remembering the total proportion of peppers shouldn't be changed.

Lemon juice can be substituted equally for lime.

CANNED WHITE POTATOES
CANNED POTATOES ARE THE SECRET TO GREAT POTATO SALAD

Since potatoes store well whole, many people don't think of canning them. However, in the spring, when even correctly stored potatoes start to sprout, you'll be glad for some canned potatoes. Canned potatoes take up less room in the cellar, too.

Small potatoes of any variety are good for canning, but they must be firm and crisp.

Canned potatoes can be used for a number of potato recipes, and because they are precooked, they can be a big time-saver. If you have ever tried to get potatoes cooked just right for potato salad, try using canned potatoes.

Canned potatoes can be used in scalloped potato recipes and as a shortcut to making casseroles, soups, and stews. *Yield: 7 quarts*

What You Will Need

20 pounds small to medium potatoes

Color preservative solution: ½ cup lemon juice mixed with ½ gallon water or ascorbic acid per label directions

Water

2½ tablespoons canning salt

7 clean, hot quart jars and lids

Pressure canner

CANNED WHITE POTATOES

Peel and slice potatoes into ½-inch rounds. Place in color preservative solution as you work to stop browning.

Drain potatoes, place in a saucepan with just enough water to cover, bring to boil, and boil 2 minutes.

Heat a saucepan of clean water (about 10 cups), add salt, and bring to a boil.

Drain potatoes, lay slices in jars to 1 inch from top. Ladle boiling salt water into jars to fill spaces, keeping a 1-inch headspace. Remove bubbles, wipe rims, top with lids, and process.

Pressure Canner Processing of Quarts for 40 minutes				
Altitude in Feet	0-2,000	2,001-4,000	4,001-6,000	6,001+
Dial Gauge	11 pounds	12 pounds	13 pounds	14 pounds
Altitude in Feet	0-1,000	1,001+		

Easy Potato Salad

To 2 quarts drained, canned potatoes, add 6 peeled and chopped hard-boiled eggs; 1 small onion, peeled and minced; and 1 cup thinly sliced celery. Blend 2 tablespoons prepared mustard with 2 cups salad dressing (Miracle Whip type), and toss until covered. If it seems dry, add more dressing. Season with salt and pepper. Chill before serving. *Yield: 2 quarts*

PREVENTING DISCOLORATION

Like some fruits, potatoes discolor when cut and exposed to air. Potatoes usually turn gray or blacken.

As you peel each potato, slice it and drop it into the color preservative solution.

Keep potato slices under the solution until you are ready to cook them. Then drain potatoes in a colander.

Even cooked potatoes will discolor if they sit too long, so be prepared to can them quickly.

FILLING JARS PROPERLY

Pack the jars tightly with slices of cooked potato. Try not to break the potatoes into small pieces. Pack one jar at a time.

Clean, boiled salt water is used to fill spaces in the jars. The tops of the potatoes should be covered with water.

Leave 1 inch of space from the top of the potatoes and water to the jar rim.

Carefully run a bubble stick around each jar and add more water if space enlarges.

CANNED SWEET POTATOES

THESE ARE CANNED IN SWEET SYRUP

Sweet potatoes are most commonly thought of as a side dish for holiday meals, but good cooks are increasingly including them in everyday meals because they are healthy and tasty.

Sweet potatoes hold their texture better when canned in syrup. You can, however, use salt water as in the recipe for Canned White Potatoes.

Sweet potatoes and yams are slightly different vegetables, but yams can be canned in the same way.

Sweet potatoes can be mashed like white potatoes, used in casseroles and soups, baked into breads and muffins, even turned into pies. Your canned sweet potatoes will make it easy to use them in all kinds of recipes. *Yield: 7 quarts*

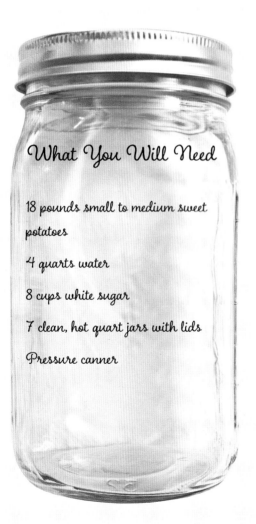

What You Will Need

18 pounds small to medium sweet potatoes

4 quarts water

8 cups white sugar

7 clean, hot quart jars with lids

Pressure canner

CANNED SWEET POTATOES

Wash sweet potatoes, place in a pot with enough water to cover, and bring to a boil.

Boil 15 minutes. Remove from heat and quickly slip off skins . Cut potatoes into chunks that will fit in jars.

Bring 4 quarts water to a boil, add sugar, and stir to dissolve. Keep water lightly boiling.

Place potatoes in jars, leaving 1-inch headspace. Ladle boiling syrup into jars to fill spaces, keeping 1-inch headspace. Remove bubbles, wipe rims, top with lids, and process.

Pressure Canner Processing of Quarts for 90 minutes				
Altitude in Feet	0-2,000	2,001-4,000	4,001-6,000	6,001+
Dial Gauge	11 pounds	12 pounds	13 pounds	14 pounds
Altitude in Feet	0-1,000	1,001+		

Sweet Potatoes

Sweet potatoes are a Native American food, although 90 percent of the world crop is now grown and consumed in Asia. American consumption is 4.6 pounds per person per year, down from 21.7 pounds in the 1940s. That's a shame because sweet potatoes are high in vitamins A and C and calcium. There are two types of sweet potatoes: yellow dry fleshed and orange moist fleshed.

REMOVING THE SKINS

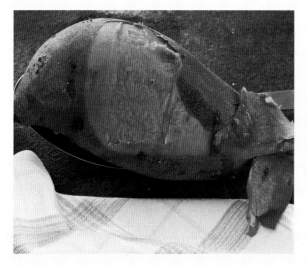

You may want to use gloves to remove the skins, because the sweet potatoes will be very hot.

After the potatoes have cooked, you should be able to push the skins off with your fingers.

It's easier to get the skins off whole potatoes than pieces, so cut potatoes after cooking.

Sweet potatoes are generally cut into chunks rather than slices. Do not mash the sweet potatoes; they would be too dense to heat properly during processing.

MAKING THE SYRUP

Heat the water in a large pan to boiling, then gradually pour in the sugar, stirring as you do so.

Stir until all the sugar is dissolved; then turn down the heat so the syrup is gently boiling.

Keep the syrup boiling while you fill the jars with potatoes. Ladle the hot syrup over them to fill the spaces.

All the pieces must be submerged in the syrup. Run a bubble stick through the jars to remove air.

CANNED CARROTS

NUTRITIOUS, COLORFUL, AND DELICIOUS, CARROTS CAN BE USED AS A SIDE DISH AND IN SOUPS AND STEWS

Carrots now come in yellow, red, purple, and white, as well as orange. While the color doesn't matter in canning, choose young, small tender carrots to can. Older, larger carrots are fibrous and may be tough when canned. Carrots for canning should be fresh and firm, not shriveled or soft.

Children are more inclined to eat carrots than other vegetables because they are colorful and mild in flavor. If children help you grow and can them, they may be even more inclined to eat them. Carrots are packed full of vitamin A and are low in calories and carbohydrates.

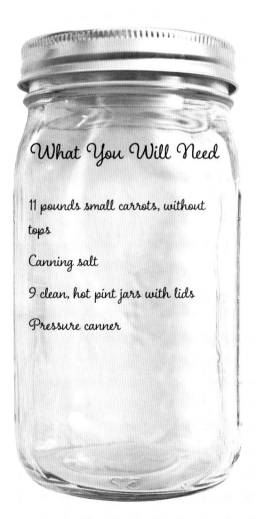

What You Will Need

11 pounds small carrots, without tops

Canning salt

9 clean, hot pint jars with lids

Pressure canner

CANNED CARROTS

Scrub and peel carrots. Wash again. Slice carrots into rounds or lengthwise into sticks, whichever you prefer.

Bring a pot of water to a boil.

Place 1 teaspoon salt in each jar. Arrange carrot pieces in jars, leaving 1-inch headspace. Ladle boiling water into each jar, maintaining the headspace.

Remove bubbles, wipe rims, top with lids, and process.

Canned carrots make it easy to include them as a side dish and to use them in soups and stews. *Yield: 9 pints*

Pressure Canner Processing of Pints for 25 minutes				
Altitude in Feet	0-2,000	2,001-4,000	4,001-6,000	6,001+
Dial Gauge	11 pounds	12 pounds	13 pounds	14 pounds
Altitude in Feet	0-1,000	1,001+		

Copper Pennies

Combine 1 cup tomato sauce, ½ cup olive oil, ¾ cup vinegar, ¾ cup packed brown sugar, and 1 tablespoon each prepared mustard and Worcestershire sauce in a saucepan over medium heat; stir until sugar melts. Peel and chop 1 small onion and 1 green pepper. Place in a bowl. Drain 2 pints canned carrots; add to bowl. Pour in liquid; refrigerate 24 hours. *Yield: 4 cups*

REMOVE ALL SOIL

Scrub carrots vigorously under water to remove all traces of soil. Soil particles can cause spoilage.

Wash carrots a second time after peeling them. Remove green shoulders and long narrow tips.

You can cut carrots in rounds or make sticks or cubes according to your preference.

Very tiny new carrots can have the shoulders and tip removed and be canned whole, without peeling, if they are scrubbed meticulously.

RAW PACKING JARS

To keep carrots from getting too soft in processing, they are not cooked before jars are packed.

Raw-packed foods shrink as they cook in processing. Jars must be packed firmly to account for this.

Salt can be omitted if desired. Boiling water is used to fill spaces in jars.

If jars don't look full enough after processing, do not open them to add more fluid. Use those jars first if they seal, or refrigerate and use them immediately.

CANNED BEETS

BEETS ARE AS QUICK AND EASY TO GROW AS THEY ARE TO CAN

Beets are another vegetable that has seen its popularity slide over the years. They are high in folic acid and great for pregnant women. They have fiber, which aids digestion, and are naturally high in many minerals like calcium, copper, and iodine, as well as antioxidants.

Beets are easy to grow, and a gardener can get several crops a year. Use the small tender roots for canning and the beet tops for a salad or cooked greens.

Canned beets can be used for a nutritious side dish, as colorful garnishes, in soups, and even in baked goods.

Beet juice is used as a safe dye for other foods. You may want to color your Easter eggs in it! *Yield: 9 pints*

What You Will Need

14 pounds small beets, 1-2 inches in diameter

Water

3 tablespoons canning salt

9 clean, hot pint jars and lids

Pressure canner

CANNED BEETS

Scrub beets and cut off tops, leaving 1 inch attached. Leave roots.

Place beats in a pot, cover with water, and bring to a boil. Boil 15 minutes.

Drain beets; allow to cool slightly. Slip off skins. Slice beets into ½-inch slices or cubes. Bring 1 quart water to a boil.

Put 1 teaspoon salt in each jar. Pack beets to 1-inch headspace. Add boiling water to fill spaces. Keep 1 inch from top. Remove bubbles, wipe rims, top with lids, and process.

Pressure Canner Processing of Pints for 30 minutes				
Altitude in Feet	0-2,000	2,001-4,000	4,001-6,000	6,001+
Dial Gauge	11 pounds	12 pounds	13 pounds	14 pounds
Altitude in Feet	0-1,000	1,001+		

Apple Beet Salad

Combine ¼ cup vinegar, ½ cup olive oil, 1 tablespoon lemon juice, 1 tablespoon honey, and ¼ teaspoon allspice in a saucepan. Heat just until boiling; cool. Drain and chop 1 pint beets. Combine with 2 cups firm, chopped apples, ¼ cup sliced green onion, and ¾ cup sliced celery. Place on salad greens, add dressing, and sprinkle with chopped walnuts. *Yield: 4-6 servings*

PREVENTING "BLEEDING"

Beets will bleed profusely during cooking. Some of the color will be retained if some of the long taproot is left on during cooking.

At least 1 inch of the long, slender taproot should be left. About 1 inch of the tops should also be left on during cooking.

Loss of juice during cooking means a lot of valuable nutrients are also lost.

After cooking, trim off roots and tops.

REMOVING THE SKINS

You may want to use gloves to skin beets, as they are hot and may stain your hands.

The beet skin should slide off with finger pressure. Use a scrubbing motion. Rubber gloves help with this.

Once skinned, cut the beets into the desired shape. Round slices or cubes can be used.

Small tender beets can be canned whole and make good garnishes.

WHOLE KERNEL CORN

CANNED CORN IS FLAVORFUL AND TENDER

Corn isn't the most nutritious vegetable we can eat, but it sure is good. If you have lots of tender sweet corn and can't eat it all fresh, consider canning some of it.

Corn comes in white, yellow, and mixed varieties. All are great for canning. For canning, you want young tender kernels, not starchy overripe ones. Use your fingernail to pierce a kernel in the middle of an ear. If the fluid is clear, it's immature; if the fluid is milky, it's just right; and if the fluid is thick and doughy, the corn is too starchy.

Canned corn makes an easy side dish, and it's good for casseroles, soups, and stews. *Yield: 9 pints*

What You Will Need

20 pounds sweet corn in the husk

Water

2 tablespoons canning salt

9 clean, hot pint jars and lids

Pressure canner

WHOLE KERNEL CORN

Husk corn and remove silk.

Working with a few ears at a time, place in boiling water for 3 minutes, remove, and cut corn from cob with cutter. Do not scrape cob.

Measure corn and place into pot. Boil some clean water. Add 1 cup boiling water for every 4 cups corn. Bring to a boil, reduce heat, and simmer 5 minutes.

Add ½ teaspoon salt to each jar. Pour corn and water into jar, leaving 1-inch headspace. Remove bubbles, wipe rims, top with lids, and process.

Pressure Canner Processing of Pints for 55 minutes			
Altitude in Feet	0-2,000	2,001-4,000	4,001-6,000	6,001+
Dial Gauge	11 pounds	12 pounds	13 pounds	14 pounds
Altitude in Feet	0-1,000	1,001+		

Corn Tips

Some varieties of corn brown slightly when canned. The color is harmless and doesn't affect the taste. This generally occurs in varieties that are high in sugar or when the corn is immature. If you have an abundance of a supersweet variety, let it mature before canning. If you grow corn, look for corn varieties that are good for canning, often noted in catalogs or on seed packets. If looks are important, test can a small amount first to see what happens.

REMOVING SILK

Silk is the white threadlike substance under the corn husk. Each piece of silk is attached to its own kernel of corn.

Peel the husk back and pull off as much silk as you can by hand.

Then dampen a rough washcloth or dish towel and run it down the ear to remove the rest of the silk.

Trim off the end of the cob where any immature kernels are and any bad spots.

REMOVING THE KERNELS

A corn cutter is a round instrument with two handles.

With the cob standing upright, place the cutter over the ear, squeeze, and push downward.

To use a knife, hold the cob at an angle. Use the stem for a handle. Then place the sharp edge of a knife on one end and slice away from you.

The kernels should be cut off at about ¾ of their depth on the cob. Don't scrape the cob after cutting.

CREAMED CORN

A SMOOTH, MOUTH-PLEASING SIDE DISH

Creamed corn is a mixture made up of pieces of whole corn and a soup of corn "milk" and kernel hearts scraped off the cob. There is no real cream or milk in it. Corn must be immature and in the "milk" stage to make good creamed corn. That means when you cut a kernel, a milky juice squirts out.

Yellow or white sweet corn can be used. Freshly picked corn has the most juice.

Canned creamed corn makes a quick side dish, or it can be used in corn bread, soups, and casseroles. Adding roasted red peppers and some real cream to canned creamed corn makes an excellent soup. *Yield: 9 pints*

What You Will Need

20 pounds sweet corn in the husk

Water

2 tablespoons canning salt (optional)

9 clean, hot jars with lids

Pressure canner

CREAMED CORN

Husk corn and remove silk.

Working with a few ears at a time, place in boiling water for 4 minutes, remove, and cut corn from the cob. Scrape cobs with a spoon.

Measure corn and scrapings and place in a pot. Boil some clean water and add 2 cups boiling water for every 4 cups of corn. Bring to a boil.

Add ½ teaspoon salt to each jar (if using) and fill with hot corn mix, leaving 1-inch headspace. Remove bubbles, wipe rims, top with lids, and process.

Pressure Canner Processing of Pints for 85 minutes				
Altitude in Feet	0-2,000	2,001-4,000	4,001-6,000	6,001+
Dial Gauge	11 pounds	12 pounds	13 pounds	14 pounds
Altitude in Feet	0-1,000	1,001+		

SCRAPING THE COBS

For creamed corn use a corn cutter or knife to cut kernels at about ½ their depth on the cob.

After the kernels are cut, use a table knife or spoon to scrape the cob. Pieces of the kernel heart and a milky fluid will be expressed.

Thoroughly blend the kernels and the milky juice you scraped out.

Then measure the corn carefully to see how much boiling water to add to the mix.

FILLING THE JARS

After adding boiling water to the creamed corn, let the mixture come to a full boil.

Add salt to the bottom of each jar if desired. The salt can be omitted.

Pour hot corn into the jars through a funnel to 1 inch from the top. Corn expands slightly in processing, so leave the extra room.

Make sure to run a bubble stick through the jar and wipe any sticky residue off the rim.

CANNED SPINACH

GREEN GOODNESS THAT MAKES A GREAT DIP

Greens are difficult to store in any fashion. However, the greens that are commonly cooked before eating can be canned. You can use this recipe to can collard and turnip greens, as well.

Choose young tender leaves, without fungal diseases or heavy insect damage. The greens should be canned shortly after they are harvested and should not be allowed to wilt before cooking.

Spinach comes in a puckered leaf variety called savoy and a smooth leaf variety. Both are good for canning.

Canned spinach can be used as a side dish or in many recipes for soups, soufflés, quiche, and pasta. Having some canned spinach on hand makes entertaining easy. It makes many excellent dips and spreads. *Yield: 9 pints*

What You Will Need

18 pounds fresh spinach

Canning salt

Water

Steamer or pot with steamer basket

9 clean, hot pint jars with lids

Pressure canner

CANNED SPINACH

Wash spinach carefully. Soak in a solution of 1 cup salt per gallon of water for 15 minutes. Drain and discard water.

Cut heavy ribs and stems from leaves. Put spinach in steamer; steam until well wilted, 3 to 5 minutes. Drain. Get 2 quarts of water boiling.

Put ½ teaspoon salt in each jar. Pack wilted greens loosely in jars, leaving 1-inch headspace. Pour boiling water in jars, maintaining headspace.

Remove bubbles, wipe rims, top with lids, and process.

Pressure Canner Processing of Pints for 70 minutes				
Altitude in Feet	0-2,000	2,001-4,000	4,001-6,000	6,001+
Dial Gauge	11 pounds	12 pounds	13 pounds	14 pounds
Altitude in Feet	0-1,000	1,001+		

Classic Spinach Dip

Drain 1 pint canned spinach and place it in a bowl. Add 1½ cups sour cream, 1 cup mayonnaise, ¼ cup thinly sliced green onions, 1 package dry vegetable soup mix, and ½ cup finely chopped water chestnuts. Blend ingredients until smooth; refrigerate, covered, for 12 hours. Serve in a hollowed bread bowl with crackers. *Yield: about 4 cups*

PROPERLY WASHING GREENS

Spinach and other greens can be tricky to wash, as the leaf folds often hide grit and insects.

Soak greens that might hold insects in cold salt water (1 cup salt per gallon) for 30 minutes.

Drain off the salt water and rinse with cold clean water. Really sandy greens may need several washings.

Inspect the leaves as you wash, discarding thick stems and ribs and rotted or diseased areas.

WILTING THE GREENS

Wilting greens is better than boiling them, as fewer nutrients are lost and the texture is better.

Place the greens in the steamer basket in small quantities. It takes 3 to 5 minutes to steam wilt the greens.

Keep steamed greens covered and warm while you steam additional batches. Properly wilted greens will look soft and dark green.

Pack greens loosely in the jars; do not tamp the spinach down. Fill spaces with boiling water. Salt can be omitted from this recipe.

CANNED PUMPKIN OR SQUASH

CANNED PUMPKIN IS GREAT FOR PIES, BAKING, OR SIDE DISHES

Pumpkins and winter squashes are pretty interchangeable in recipes. In fact, commercially canned pumpkin is actually from a tan-colored squash. Mature winter squash and pumpkins have a thick outer skin, called the rind, which allows them to be stored for quite some time in a warm, dark spot.

Since pumpkin and squash take a bit of preparation to be suitable for cooking, having canned pumpkin or squash on hand is a big time-saver.

Canned pumpkin and squash are not only for pies. They are used in main dishes like soups and stews and as a side dish.

What You Will Need

18 pounds mature pumpkin or squash with hard rinds (pie-type pumpkins give best results)

Water

7 clean, hot quart jars and lids (widemouthed jars work well)

Pressure canner

CANNED PUMPKIN OR SQUASH

Scrub the outside of the pumpkins to remove any dirt. Split the pumpkins and remove seeds and pulp.

Cut the pumpkin flesh into 1-inch chunks and slice off the outer rind. Place the chunks in a pot of water and bring to a boil. Boil 3 minutes.

Use tongs to place chunks in jars. Pour hot cooking water over the chunks, leaving 1-inch headspace. Do not mash chunks.

Remove bubbles, wipe rims, top with lids, and process.

Pumpkins and squash should be fully ripe and firm for canning. Frosted or frozen pumpkin and squash should not be used. *Yield: 7 quarts*

Pressure Canner Processing of Quarts for 90 minutes				
Altitude in Feet	0-2,000	2,001-4,000	4,001-6,000	6,001+
Dial Gauge	11 pounds	12 pounds	13 pounds	14 pounds
Altitude in Feet	0-1,000	1,001+		

Pumpkin and Squash

Pumpkins and squash are native to the Americas. In earlier times they were cut in chunks and smoked or dried for preservation as well as stored whole inside the home. The seeds were carefully saved and roasted for a treat. As the story goes, pioneers hollowed out pumpkins, filled them with milk and a little sugar, and then set them to roast in a fire—the precursor to pumpkin pie.

CLEANING AND CUTTING UP PUMPKIN

Cleaning a pumpkin is quite messy. Protect your work surface and have something handy to dispose of the unwanted "goo" inside.

Slice the pumpkin in half and remove the seeds and pulp. You can save the seeds to roast if you wish.

Scrape the walls of the pumpkin clean with a spoon. Then cut the pumpkin into chunks.

Carefully stand a chunk on end and slice off the outer rind. There is a color change between the rind and the flesh.

PREPARING PUMPKIN FOR RECIPES

For canning, you want to leave the pumpkin in chunks about 1-inch thick. Don't mash or puree the pumpkin before canning.

Mashed pumpkin will not heat properly in the canner and may spoil. Chunks also allow versatility in later uses.

It's easy to puree or blend canned pumpkin chunks in a blender of food processor, or you can use a potato masher.

Spices are easily blended into mashed or pureed pumpkin. Excess mashed pumpkin can be frozen.

CANNED PEAS WITH PEARLS

A SPRING-INSPIRED SIDE DISH THAT'S SURE TO PLEASE

Peas grow best in cool weather, in early spring over most of the country. Even a small patch can give you more peas than you can eat fresh. At this time of year there are few other things to can, so the peas can get your full attention.

Peas for canning should be young and small. Use only peas that you shell out of the pod, not peas in edible pods for canning.

This recipe combines two spring favorites: small onions and peas. The flavors are a good blend and reminiscent of spring any time of the year. If you can't find the small onions, the peas can be canned without them.

This recipe can easily be frozen. *Yield: 9 pints*

What You Will Need

16 pounds peas in pods

6 cups tiny white onions, less than 1 inch in diameter

Water

Strainer or colander

3 tablespoons canning salt (optional)

9 clean, hot pint jars and lids

Pressure canner

CANNED PEAS WITH PEARLS

Shell peas. Working with small batches, dip onions in boiling water, then cold, and slip off skins. Cut off roots.

Place whole, peeled onions in a pot, cover with water, and bring to a boil; boil 3 minutes. Add peas and additional water to cover, bring to a boil; boil 2 minutes.

Place ½ teaspoon salt (if using) in each jar. Loosely fill with peas and onions; add cooking water, leaving 1-inch headspace.

Remove bubbles, wipe rims, top with lids, and process.

Pressure Canner Processing of Pints for 40 minutes			
Altitude in Feet	0-2,000	2,001-4,000	4,001-6,000	6,001+
Dial Gauge	11 pounds	12 pounds	13 pounds	14 pounds
Altitude in Feet	0-1,000	1,001+		
Weight Gauge	10 pounds	15 pounds		

Onion Tips

Small onions are sometimes for sale in gourmet markets. You can purchase seeds to grow your own pearl-type onions, sometimes called pickling onions, but an easy substitute is the small Dutch onion sets sold in early spring. Choose white sets (tiny bulbs) and look for the more rounded ones. The sets are often sold in bulk, which allows you to pick the perfect size and shaped bulbs.

PEELING THE PEARLS

Work with a few onions at a time. Place onions in a strainer or small colander, dip in boiling water, then dip quickly into cold water.

Push the papery onion skins, which will now be soft, back toward the root end of the onion.

With a sharp knife, trim off the root pad just above the skins you pushed back; discard the skins.

Leave the tip on the onion, as it will help hold the onion layers together. Trim any skin off the top.

PACKING PEAS AND PEARLS

Don't overcook the peas and onions; they should still be firm when you pack them. Add salt to each jar, if desired.

Lift the onions from the pot with a slotted spoon and try to divide them evenly among the jars.

Use a slotted spoon and a jar funnel to get peas into the jars. Pack loosely to 1 inch from rim.

Make sure all peas and onions are completely covered by cooking water in the jar before processing.

CANNED GREEN BEANS
EASY TO GROW, EASY TO CAN, AND GREAT EATING YEAR-ROUND

The second most popular item to can is probably green beans. They are easy for gardeners to grow and easy to find in farmers' markets. They are usually available all summer.

Choose tender, thin young beans. Older beans are tough and tasteless. Beans can be various shades of green or purple or mottled. Purple beans usually turn green when cooked.

"Stringless" varieties are popular in home gardens, but older "string" beans may have a richer bean flavor. The string should be pulled off the pod before cutting the beans.

Yellow wax beans are canned just like green beans. And yellow and green beans can be mixed for pretty jars.

What You Will Need

9 pounds green beans

Water

3 tablespoons canning salt (optional)

9 clean, hot pint jars with lids

Pressure canner

CANNED GREEN BEANS

Go through beans and discard those that look discolored, moldy, or bug eaten. Select young, tender pods with small beans inside.

Wash beans and trim off both ends. Cut or "snap" beans if desired.

Place beans in pot with enough water to cover. Bring to a boil and boil 5 minutes. Remove from heat.

Put ½ teaspoon salt (if using) in each jar. Fill with beans and cooking water, leaving 1-inch headspace. Remove bubbles, wipe rims, top with lids, and process.

Green beans can be served as a simple side dish or as part of an elaborate party casserole. *Yield: 9 pints*

Pressure Canner Processing of Pints for 20 minutes				
Altitude in Feet	0-2,000	2,001-4,000	4,001-6,000	6,001+
Dial Gauge	11 pounds	12 pounds	13 pounds	14 pounds
Altitude in Feet	0-1,000	1,001+		
Weight Gauge	10 pounds	15 pounds		

Green Bean Casserole

Drain 2 pints canned beans. Combine 1 can condensed cream of mushroom soup, ½ cup milk, and ⅛ teaspoon black pepper; stir until smooth. Add ¾ cup fried onion rings and the beans and stir. Transfer to a casserole dish; bake at 350°F 25 minutes. Remove and top with 2 cups cheddar cheese shreds and onion rings; return to oven 5 minutes. *Yield: 6 servings*

WAYS TO CUT BEANS

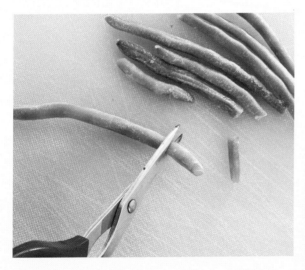

Some people simply snap beans into pieces. They can also be cut with a knife or kitchen shears. Beans can be left whole if small.

French-style beans are cut into narrow strips down the length of the bean.

"Frenching," or shredding, beans can be done with a knife, but a special machine makes it easier.

You can find bean cutters at specialty stores, and some food processors have adaptors or built-in shredders.

FILLING THE JARS

Salt can be omitted or reduced in this recipe.

Pack beans loosely in jars, as some swelling occurs in processing. Shake jars gently to settle pieces.

Leave the required 1-inch headspace at the top of the jars, but make sure all the beans are covered with cooking fluid.

Make sure to run a bubble stick through the beans and along the jar sides and adjust fluid if needed.

CANNED BEANS

HERE'S HOW TO CAN LIMA, BLACK, NAVY, KIDNEY, AND OTHER BEANS

Beans store well dried, but having some cooked canned beans can be a big time-saver in the kitchen.

Beans that are dried can be soaked overnight in two changes of water, boiled for 30 minutes, and then canned. Alternatively, beans can be picked fresh and shelled for canning. Fresh beans should be mature, with the pods just starting to dry. The beans inside should still feel soft.

There are dozens of types of shell beans, from pintos to old heirloom soup beans. All can be canned.

Beans are extremely versatile in the kitchen and a source of protein for vegetarian meals. A whole meal can be made from beans, or they can be served as a side dish. *Yield: 9 pints*

What You Will Need

18 pounds beans in the shell (not dried)

Water

1½ tablespoons canning salt

9 clean, hot pint jars and lids

Pressure canner

CANNED BEANS

Shell beans and wash thoroughly.

Place beans in a large pot of water and bring to a boil. Boil 1 minute.

Put ½ teaspoon salt in each jar. Fill jars with hot beans; add some cooking water. Leave 1 inch space to rim.

Remove bubbles, wipe rims, top with lids, and process.

Pressure Canner Processing of Pints for 40 minutes			
Altitude in Feet	0-2,000	2,001-4,000	4,001-6,000	6,001+
Dial Gauge	11 pounds	12 pounds	13 pounds	14 pounds
Altitude in Feet	0-1,000	1,001+		
Weight Gauge	10 pounds	15 pounds		

Best Baked Beans

Brown 1 pound ground meat and 1 small onion, chopped. Drain grease. Drain 2 pints navy or other soup beans, saving 1 cup liquid. In a large casserole, mix ½ cup packed brown sugar, 1 cup catsup, 1 teaspoon seasoned salt, ¼ teaspoon black pepper, and reserved bean juice. Stir in meat and beans. Bake at 350°F 1 hour, until thick. *Yield: 6 servings*

SHELLING BEANS

Squeeze a pod between your fingers and it will generally pop open; if not, snip off the tip and use your finger to open. Limas may need to be cut down the side.

Use your thumb to rake out the beans and drop them into a container. This should go fast and easy.

Periodically sort through the beans and remove any that look underdeveloped or moldy or have insect holes.

Make sure to wash the beans after shelling.

LEAVE ENOUGH SPACE

Beans are very apt to swell during cooking and push the fluid under the seals, preventing a good seal.

Pack beans loosely in jars, never tamp them down. Shake jars gently to settle beans.

Leave an inch of space at the top of the jars, between the beans and the rim.

Use a bubble stick to dislodge air before processing. If jars don't seal, refrigerate the beans and use immediately.

VEGETABLE SOUP MIX
COMBINE YOUR FAVORITE VEGETABLES FOR A CUSTOM BLEND

What could be better than a bowl of steamy hot soup or stew on a cold winter day? Combine it with a loaf of homemade bread and you have a feast.

This recipe is a good way to use up small amounts of vegetables and to have a quick start for making hearty soups or stews. You can omit some vegetables if you increase the others, but be sure you always use 26 cups of vegetables.

If you add meat and thick gravy to these vegetables, it's a stew. If you add broth and noodles, it's soup; you could add chicken, beef, or other meat to the soup, too.

Make sure the vegetables are fresh and of top quality. Peel and cut as required. *Yield: 7 quarts*

What You Will Need

6 cups small white potatoes, sliced or whole

6 cups peeled, sliced carrots

6 cups cut whole kernel corn

6 cups cut green beans

4 cups shelled peas

1 cup diced onion

1 cup diced red sweet pepper

2 quarts tomato juice or water

3 tablespoons canning salt (optional)

7 clean, hot quart jars and lids

Pressure canner

VEGETABLE SOUP MIX

Prepare vegetables by washing, peeling, and cutting; keep pieces to about 1-inch thick. If potatoes are left whole, they must be 1 inch or less across.

Place all the vegetables in a large pan with enough tomato juice or water to cover. Bring to a boil; boil 5 minutes.

Add 1 teaspoon salt to each jar, if desired.

Fill jars with hot vegetables and cooking fluid to 1 inch from top. Remove bubbles, wipe rims, top with lids, and process.

Pressure Canner Processing of Pints for 90 minutes				
Altitude in Feet	0-2,000	2,001-4,000	4,001-6,000	6,001+
Dial Gauge	11 pounds	12 pounds	13 pounds	14 pounds
Altitude in Feet	0-1,000	1,001+		
Weight Gauge	10 pounds	15 pounds		

COOKING THE VEGETABLES

SOME VEGETABLE SUBSTITUTIONS

Using tomato juice to cook the vegetables gives them a better flavor.

Try to keep pieces less than 1-inch thick so vegetables cook evenly.

Salt can be omitted or reduced in this recipe, but do not use salt substitutes.

To see if vegetables are cooked correctly, test carrots or potatoes. They should be slightly soft but not falling apart.

Turnips can be substituted for potatoes or carrots. Rutabagas could be used, but they may develop a strong flavor that overpowers the mix.

Green peppers or any sweet pepper can be substituted for the red peppers. If hot peppers are used, reduce the quantity.

Chopped tomatoes can be substituted for any vegetable.

Okra can be used as a substitute for one of the vegetables. Peeled and chopped zucchini can also be used.

KOSHER DILL PICKLES
CRUNCHY, SOUR PICKLES MADE THE EASY WAY

Dill pickles are the perfect complement to any number of sandwiches, and some people love to munch on the sour, crisp treats between meals, too.

While some dill pickles are fermented in crocks for many weeks, this recipe is for a quick pickle, one that you can get canned in one day, although the flavor will be better if you let them sit for several weeks after they are canned before eating them.

The word *kosher* is generally a label for foods prepared under Jewish religious law. But when referring to pickles, it often means a pickle that has garlic added. If you truly need pickles prepared under strict kosher law, see your religious leader for guidance. *Yield: 7 pints*

What You Will Need

8 pounds pickling cucumbers, 3–4 inches long

7 clean, hot pint jars and lids

14 dill flower heads or 5 tablespoons dill seed

2½ tablespoons mustard seed

14 peppercorns

5 garlic cloves, minced

3 cups white vinegar

3 cups water

6 tablespoons pickling salt

Water-bath canner

KOSHER DILL PICKLES

Wash cucumbers. Cut off blossom end and discard. Cut into spears that fit ½ inch below rim of jars.

In each hot jar, place 1 dill flower head, or 1½ teaspoons dill seed, ½ teaspoon mustard seed, and 2 peppercorns. Divide garlic among jars.

Place spears into jars; add 1 dill flower head to middle of each jar.

Bring vinegar, water, and salt to a boil. Pour over spears to ½ inch from rim. Remove bubbles, wipe rims, place lids, and process.

Water-Bath Canner Processing Times for Pints				
Altitude in Feet	0-1,000	1,001-3,000	3,001-6,000	6,001+
Processing Time	10 minutes	15 minutes	15 minutes	20 minutes

Growing Dill

Dill is easily grown in the garden; in fact once you sow the seeds, you will probably have dill coming up in your garden for many years. If you don't have dill in your garden, the flower stalks are often sold at farmers' markets and in the produce section in grocery stores. If you can't find the dill flower heads, dill seeds are available in the spice section of grocery stores.

PREPARING THE JARS

Dill flowers that are still yellow are prettiest in the jars. Place a dill flower head in the bottom of each jar.

Put the other spices on the bottom of the jars according to recipe directions.

Pack the spears in the jars as tightly as possible, leaving ½ inch at the top.

When most of the spears are packed in the jar, place the second dill flower head against the jar side, halfway up the jar.

ADDING THE BRINE

Bring the vinegar-salt solution to a boil. Do not reduce the salt and vinegar in this recipe.

Pour the boiling solution over the spears in the jars. It's important to cover the spears completely.

After the jars are filled, run a bubble stick through the jar—there will be lots of bubbles.

If some jars don't look full after processing, don't open them unless they didn't seal. Use those jars first.

SWEET PICKLES

SWEET-AND-SOUR TIDBITS TO PLEASE THE PALATE

These pickles are both sour and sweet, a pleasing combination. This recipe does not use cloves, but you could add a small amount of cloves if you like the flavor. This is a quick pickle recipe, finished in 24 hours. They do taste better if allowed to sit for several weeks before opening and tasting them.

Sweet pickles are used on some sandwiches, and they are served as appetizers and relishes. They also make good garnishes for plates. The recipe calls for them to be cut into rounds, but they could also be cut into sticks. Very tiny cucumbers can be left whole like gherkins. (Gherkins are not cucumbers.) Make sure to remove a slice from the blossom end. *Yield: 8 pints*

What You Will Need

8 pounds pickling cucumbers

⅓ cup pickling salt

Crushed or small cubes of ice

3½ cups cider vinegar

4 cups brown sugar

2 tablespoons mustard seed

2 teaspoons celery seed

1 tablespoon whole allspice

8 sterilized pint jars and lids

Hot water canner

SWEET PICKLES

Wash cucumbers, remove blossom end, and slice into ¼-inch rounds. Place in large bowl, sprinkle salt on top, cover with ice, and refrigerate 4 hours. Replace ice as needed.

Place vinegar, sugar and spices in a saucepan; heat until boiling.

Drain cucumbers and pack into jars to ½ inch from rim. Immediately pour hot vinegar solution over slices, leaving ½ inch to rim.

Remove bubbles, wipe rims, place lids, and process. To develop flavor, allow pickles to sit 1 month before eating.

Water-Bath Canner Processing Times for Pints				
Altitude in Feet	0-1,000	1,001-3,000	3,001-6,000	6,001+
Processing Time	10 minutes	15 minutes	15 minutes	20 minutes

Limed Cucumbers

Cucumbers are sometimes limed to make crisper pickles. Use only food-grade, powdered lime, found with pickling supplies. Use 1 cup pickling lime and ½ cup salt to 1 gallon of water. Soak sliced cucumbers 12 hours, remove, rinse, and soak in fresh water 1 hour. Repeat rinse-and-soak cycle 3 times. It's extremely important to rinse the lime out for food safety. Proceed with recipe.

CRISPING PICKLES

This recipe uses an ice crisping technique. Sprinkle pickling salt on top of the pickles in a nonmetallic bowl.

Then cover the bowl with ice and put it into the refrigerator. Replace ice as needed and drain off excess water.

Leave the cucumbers in the ice for 4 hours. After that, remove and drain them well and immediately proceed with the recipe.

Always remove the blossom end from the cucumber and discard it. It softens pickles if you leave it.

MAKING THE SYRUP

You can substitute white sugar for the brown in this recipe, but the flavor will be slightly different.

Do not reduce the sugar or vinegar in this recipe. You can reduce or omit the spices as desired.

Pack the cucumber slices into the jars to within ½ inch from jar rim.

Boil the vinegar and spices, then slowly stir in the sugar. Stir until the sugar is dissolved. Pour boiling solution over pickles, completely covering them.

PICKLED PEPPER RINGS

MEDIUM HOT AND SPICY, THESE ARE A GREAT ADDITION TO THE RELISH TRAY

Besides being a tongue twister, pickled peppers make a good side dish or even an attractive gift. If you are a fire-eater, you can concentrate on hot peppers, but most people enjoy a mixture of mild and hot peppers. Even a few hot peppers in any pickle mix will raise the heat level.

Different countries and cultures have different preferences when it comes to peppers, and there are thousands of types of peppers. This recipe uses two common peppers—jalapeño and yellow banana—but you can substitute any other peppers. A blend of different colored interesting peppers makes for attractive as well as tasty jars. Just don't exceed 3 pounds of peppers in this recipe. *Yield: 6 pints*

What You Will Need

Plastic or rubber gloves

1½ pounds jalapeño peppers

1½ pounds yellow banana peppers

6 clean, hot pint jars and lids

6 tablespoons mustard seed

3 tablespoons celery seed

2 cloves garlic, finely minced

1¾ cups water

7½ cups cider vinegar

2½ tablespoons canning salt

Water-bath canner

PICKLED PEPPER RINGS

Wearing gloves, wash peppers. Remove stem end and discard. Slice peppers into rings ¼-inch thick.

Place evenly 1 tablespoon mustard seed, 1½ teaspoons celery seed, and garlic in each jar. Pack jars loosely with pepper rings, leaving ½ inch to rim.

Bring water, vinegar, and salt to a boil. Ladle over peppers in jars to ½ inch from rim.

Remove bubbles, wipe rims, place lids, and process.

Water-Bath Canner Processing Times for Pints				
Altitude in Feet	0–1,000	1,001–3,000	3,001–6,000	6,001+
Processing Time	10 minutes	15 minutes	15 minutes	20 minutes

Pepper Heat Index

The heat in peppers is measured by the **Scoville scale**, with the highest numbers having the most heat. The scale ranges from 0 to about 600,000 units. Sweet bell peppers are at the low end, and jalapeños and serranos somewhere in the middle. Habañero, chile, Thai, and Tepin are at the high end of the scale. The heat can also vary according to the ripeness of the pepper.

PREPARING PEPPERS

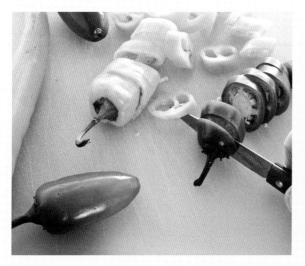

Hot peppers can burn your skin or eyes. Wear gloves when cleaning and keep your hands away from your face.

Use a sharp blade to slice peppers evenly. Remove any white membrane in the center of slices.

Try to remove as many seeds as possible; rinsing the slices helps wash away seeds.

If you want very crisp pepper rings, they can be limed after slicing. Follow the directions on page 127.

FILLING THE JARS

Since this recipe calls for peppers by weight, you may end up with more or less slices needed to fill 6 pints.

Don't can less than a full jar, and don't overfill jars to use slices. Use the extra peppers fresh or discard them.

Measure and add the spices to the bottom of each jar. Then loosely fill jars with peppers. Lay the slices flat.

Pour the hot vinegar solution over the slices, making sure all peppers are covered.

SAUERKRAUT

SAUERKRAUT TAKES TIME TO FERMENT BEFORE CANNING

For this recipe you will need time and patience. But if you love good sauerkraut, it's worth the wait. You'll need an undisturbed location for your fermenting sauerkraut, where the temperature is ideally 70°F to 75°F. At that temperature it will take 3 to 4 weeks for the sauerkraut to ferment.

Sauerkraut is canned after fermenting so it can be stored safely. You can also refrigerate it in tightly covered containers for several months.

For the best sauerkraut, use freshly harvested cabbage. Don't use old heads that have been stored for weeks. You can use red cabbage, but green looks nicer when the kraut is finished.

Sauerkraut is generally used as a side dish with pork and other meats. *Yield: About 9 quarts*

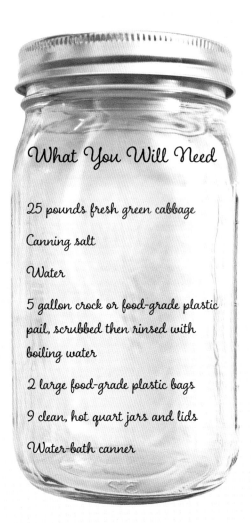

What You Will Need

25 pounds fresh green cabbage

Canning salt

Water

5 gallon crock or food-grade plastic pail, scrubbed then rinsed with boiling water

2 large food-grade plastic bags

9 clean, hot quart jars and lids

Water-bath canner

SAUERKRAUT

Wash and quarter cabbage. Mix 1 cup salt with 1 gallon water; soak cabbage for 30 minutes; drain.

Slice cabbage. Toss 10 cups with 3 tablespoons salt and pack firmly into crock. Repeat until cabbage is 5 inches from rim.

Boil 6 tablespoons salt in 1 gallon water; cool. Cover cabbage with salt water; weigh down.

Ferment cabbage at 70°F. After fermentation is complete, pack into jars to ½ inch from rim, remove bubbles, wipe rim, place lids, and process.

Water-Bath Canner Processing Times for Quarts				
Altitude in Feet	0–1,000	1,001–3,000	3,001–6,000	6,001+
Processing Time	25 minutes	30 minutes	35 minutes	40 minutes

CUTTING AND PACKING CABBAGE

After removing the core, slice cabbage into shreds less than a ¼-inch thick. Use a sharp knife or a slicing machine.

Toss cabbage slices with salt. Then put the cabbage in the crock, packing it down firmly with your hands.

After packing cabbage, pour in brine until cabbage is covered by 1 to 2 inches.

Double two large food-grade plastic bags. Fill them halfway with more brine (in case of leaks). Place the bags on top of the crock lid.

FERMENTING PROCESS

Cabbage must remain under the brine at all times. The bags of brine weigh down and cover the cabbage, keeping it under the brine.

Fermentation should begin in 24 hours and produces small bubbles in the kraut.

Check daily, and remove any scum that forms on the brine surface. Add fresh boiled and cooled brine if the level drops to expose kraut.

Fermentation can take 30 days. Kraut is finished when it is translucent and bubbling has ceased.

PERKY PICKLED BEETS

THESE ARE SWEET-AND-SOUR, A GREAT SIDE DISH, AND NUTRITIOUS, TOO

Pickled beets are an old-time favorite, often served with special meals. They are sometimes called Harvard beets. They add color and spice to the plate.

Most beets are deep red, but you can use golden or white beets in this recipe for a different look. Don't try to mix colors though; the red will color the lighter ones. If you use lighter beets, replace the brown sugar with white.

You can dice the beets in cubes, or use a slicing attachment on a food processor to make wavy or plain rounds.

The spices in this recipe can be adjusted to your

What You Will Need

7 pounds small beets, 2–2½ inches in diameter

3 medium onions

4 cups cider vinegar

2 cups brown sugar

1½ teaspoons canning salt

2 cups water

1 teaspoon cinnamon

½ teaspoon allspice

12 whole cloves

6-inch square cheesecloth or tea ball

8 clean, hot pint jars and lids

Water-bath canner

PERKY PICKLED BEETS

Wash beets; leave 1 inch of tops and roots. Cover with water and boil 30 minutes.

Remove beets; cool. Remove skin. Cut off tops and roots. Slice into ¼-inch pieces. Peel and dice onions.

Place beets, onions, vinegar, sugar, salt, and water in pot. Add spices tied in cheesecloth or tea ball. Bring to boil; simmer 5 minutes.

Discard spices. Fill jars with vegetables and hot solution; leave ½ inch headspace. Remove bubbles, wipe rims, place lids, process.

personal taste. Onions can also be left out, if you prefer. Don't change the sugar and vinegar amounts, however. *Yield: 8 pints*

Water-Bath Canner Processing Times for Pints				
Altitude in Feet	0-1,000	1,001-3,000	3,001-6,000	6,001+
Processing Time	30 minutes	35 minutes	40 minutes	45 minutes

Healthy Beets

While this recipe is high in sugar, it does feature a vegetable with lots of health benefits. Beets are high in antioxidants and dietary fiber. They are a good source of folic acid, vitamin C, iron, and potassium. Children usually eat them; especially in a sweet-and-sour pickle form, because they are different looking and milder in flavor than most vegetables. Pickled beets make an edible garnish.

COOKING AND PREPARING BEETS

Leaving the long taproot and 1 inch of the top when cooking beets will keep them from losing juice and valuable nutrients.

After cooking you should be able to easily pull off the skins.

Trim off the taproot and top after cooking and discard. Discard the cooking water, too.

Dice the beets or slice them into rounds. Beets may stain your hands or clothes. You may want to wear gloves and an apron.

ADDING THE SPICES

A metal tea ball works well for adding spices. Put in the spices and hang it on the pot side.

Or put your spices in the center of a piece of cheesecloth, and tie a knot in it or tie it with a piece of string.

Float the tea ball or cheesecloth packet in the simmering mixture to flavor the onions and beets.

After simmering, remove and discard the spices. This keeps hard spice pieces out of the jars.

FIESTA PICKLED VEGETABLES

A COLORFUL DISH WITH ENOUGH ZIP TO INSPIRE PICKY EATERS

These beautiful pickled mixed vegetables make an excellent holiday side dish or a delightful gift in a nicely decorated jar. Even your vegetable hater will enjoy this flavorful dish. This recipe makes enough for home and gifts.

If you don't like the taste of certain spices, you can eliminate them. You can also substitute or leave out one or more vegetables, but be careful to maintain the ratio of about 24 cups of vegetables to the salt-vinegar solution. Sliced, small zucchini can be substituted for some or all of the cucumbers. Be conscious of maintaining a colorful blend, as that is part of the charm of this dish. *Yield: 10 pints*

What You Will Need

10 cups sliced, small pickling cucumbers
4 large carrots
2 pounds small onions
8–12 stalks celery
2–3 red peppers
1 head cauliflower
5 cups white vinegar
¼ cup prepared mustard
½ cup pickling salt
3½ cups brown sugar
3 tablespoons celery seed
2 tablespoons mustard seed
½ teaspoon whole cloves
½ teaspoon turmeric
10 sterilized pint jars
Water-bath canner

FIESTA PICKLED VEGETABLES

Wash all vegetables. Peel the carrots and onions; slice or dice all vegetables into ½-inch pieces. Discard blossom end of cucumber. Place vegetables in bowl, cover with ice, and refrigerate 4 hours.

Place remaining ingredients in a large pot. Bring to a boil, stirring to blend.

Drain vegetables, add to pot, and return to a boil. Turn off heat. Quickly pack vegetables into sterile jars; add cooking brine to ½ inch from rim.

Remove bubbles, wipe rims, place lids, and process.

MAKE IT EASY

There are many fancy cut-glass or embossed canning jars on the market that you can buy to turn your canned items into pretty gifts. Process the food in those jars; don't transfer it. Add squares of pretty fabric to the tops, tied on with bits of ribbon or raffia. Make sure to include a label. The label should list the ingredients, so the recipient can check for allergy-inducing items.

ADDING VEGETABLES

PACKING FOR COLOR

Notice that the cucumbers are not peeled in this recipe, but make sure to remove the blossom end.

Very small onions that are left whole look best in this recipe.

Use a spoon to gently push the vegetables out of a colander held close to the brine surface. Dumping them in may cause hot liquid to splash on you.

Do not overcook the vegetables, or they will be soft. As soon as the liquid boils after adding vegetables, turn off the heat.

Make sure jars are sterilized and kept hot before filling. Keep pickling mix simmering hot, too.

For the best appearance, cut vegetables in even-size pieces and mix varieties well in the jars.

You may want to use small tongs to arrange vegetables with an eye to color, so carrots and peppers are evenly distributed.

Pack vegetables tightly and run a bubble stick around the sides and through the jar before processing to reduce shrinkage.

TOMATO KETCHUP

KETCHUP IS AMERICA'S FAVORITE CONDIMENT; YOURS CAN BE HOMEMADE

Ketchup is used on nearly everything, from fried potatoes to fried eggs. The flavor of ketchup varies, and in this recipe you are free to vary the spices to suit your taste.

If you are amazed at the amount of sugar in this recipe, look at the label of commercial ketchups. Most of them use corn syrup for a sweetener, but it's as sweet as this homemade version. The sugar helps thicken the ketchup. The salt can be left out or reduced without harm.

If your family balks at ketchup in a pint jar, you can pour the ketchup into one of those plastic dispensers just before use. Keep opened jars of homemade ketchup in the refrigerator. *Yield: About 9 pints*

What You Will Need

24–25 pounds tomatoes (paste type is best)
8 large sweet red bell peppers
6 large onions
Food processor or strainer
9 cups vinegar
9 cups sugar
½ cup canning salt
3 tablespoons celery seed
3 tablespoons dry mustard
1 teaspoon black pepper
1 tablespoon whole cloves
½ teaspoon powdered cinnamon
½ teaspoon garlic powder
¼ teaspoon allspice
6-inch square cheesecloth or spice bag
9 clean, hot pint jars and lids
Water-bath canner

TOMATO KETCHUP

Wash tomatoes, peel (see page 89), chop. Wash peppers, remove seeds, chop. Peel and dice onions.

Blend vegetables in food processor until smooth. Or cook them 20 minutes and push through strainer.

Put vegetables in a pot; slowly boil for 60 minutes. Combine spices in cheesecloth or ball and add all ingredients to the pot. Cook, stirring frequently, until very thick.

Remove spices; pour ketchup into jars to ⅛ inch from rim. Wipe rims, place lids, process.

Water-Bath Canner Processing Times for Pints				
Altitude in Feet	0-1,000	1,001-3,000	3,001-6,000	6,001+
Processing Time	15 minutes	20 minutes	20 minutes	25 minutes

A Quick History

Ketchup or catsup was originally a word used for a sauce made out of a number of things: walnuts, mushrooms, even fish. They were salty and bitter. When Americans began to use tomatoes, in the early 1800s, ketchup became a name for a tomato-based condiment that has become increasingly thicker and sweeter. In the Philippines, ketchup is made from bananas and colored red.

ADDING SPICES

Spices are added to the cooking tomatoes in a tied cheesecloth square, spice bag, or tea ball.

This helps you to avoid the messy job of straining whole spices out of the sauce.

You could add powdered spices directly to the sauce, but the celery seed and cloves need to be in a ball or bag.

The spices in the recipe will give you a ketchup flavor similar to commercial ketchups, but you can vary the spices to suit your taste.

CHOOSE YOUR THICKNESS

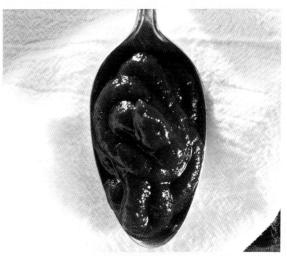

Originally ketchup was thin and watery. Most people prefer a thicker sauce now.

Using paste-type tomatoes makes the sauce thicker faster. Do not reduce the vinegar in the recipe.

The longer you cook the sauce, the more water evaporates and the thicker it becomes. Stir frequently to prevent scorching.

Ketchup is considered done when it mounds on a spoon. You can stop when it's thinner if you like.

QUICK HOT SAUCE
THIS KICKY SAUCE USES YOUR CANNED (OR PURCHASED) TOMATOES

One person's hot sauce can be a bland sauce to another. This recipe makes a fairly hot sauce, but you can adjust the types of peppers used in it to make it hotter or milder.

This is an easy recipe to make, but it will make you look like a cooking master as you serve it with meats, eggs, or other dishes. If you don't have canned tomatoes, you can buy commercially canned diced tomatoes to use in the recipe.

You can also experiment with spices in this recipe to get something unique. Once you have perfected the recipe, can it and give it as gifts.

Make sure to refrigerate any opened jars of home-made hot sauce. *Yield: About 4 half-pint jars*

What You Will Need

Plastic or rubber gloves

1½ cups chopped hot peppers (use serrano, jalapeño, Tabasco, cayenne, or a mixture)

8 cups diced, canned tomatoes, undrained

4 cups cider vinegar

2 teaspoons canning salt

2 tablespoons store-bought pickling spice

¼ teaspoon garlic powder

¼ teaspoon onion powder

Spice bag, tea ball, or 6-inch square cheesecloth

Food processor or blender

4 clean, hot half-pint jars and lids

Water-bath canner

QUICK HOT SAUCE

Wearing gloves, wash peppers and remove cores and seeds. Chop finely.

Measure peppers and tomatoes; place in pot. Add vinegar and salt. Tie spices in a bag or cheesecloth or put in tea ball; add to pot.

Bring to a boil, then simmer 20 minutes. Remove spices. Place mixture in processor or blender and blend until smooth. Return to pot and boil 15 minutes, stirring frequently.

Pour into jars to ¼ inch from rim. Wipe rims, place lids, and process.

Water-Bath Canner Processing Times for Half-Pints				
Altitude in Feet	0-1,000	1,001-3,000	3,001-6,000	6,001+
Processing Time	10 minutes	15 minutes	15 minutes	20 minutes

MAKE IT EASY

You can find premixed pickling spices in little bottles and packets in the spice section of good stores. Because only a small amount of various spices are needed, this is an economical way to buy pickling spices. Choose a blend without dill for this recipe. Don't use leftover mixes for spaghetti sauce or other dishes, as the flavor is meant for the pickling process.

ADDING SPICES

The salt, garlic powder, and onion powder in this recipe can be directly added to the cooking sauce.

Pickling spices generally have large, whole spice pieces in them. They need to be contained in a packet or ball for easy removal.

Or you could use your own blend of powdered spices and add them directly to the cooking sauce.

Suggested spices are black pepper, cayenne pepper, chili powder, cloves, cinnamon, celery seed, horseradish, mustard seed, all spice, bay leaves, and cumin.

BLENDING THE SAUCE

Hot sauce should be very smooth, with no pieces of visible vegetables.

Using a blender or food processor is the best way to puree the vegetables smooth.

Alternately you could use a potato masher and a whisk and blend the sauce smooth by hand.

Hot sauce is thinner than ketchup. If it isn't thick enough for your taste, you can cook it longer to evaporate more water.

SWEET PICKLE RELISH
EXCELLENT ON HOT DOGS OR IN TUNA SALAD

Pickle relish is used directly on foods like hot dogs and sausages or mixed into salads. Tuna salad, egg salad, and potato salad benefit from a little sweet pickle relish.

Relish is a good place to use older cucumbers and cucumbers meant for the table, although pickling cucumbers make a premium product. All cucumbers you use should be fresh and firm—the fresher the better. You don't peel the cucumbers in this recipe; make sure they are very clean before using.

This is a common cucumber relish, but all kinds of interesting relishes exist. There are a couple of additional relish recipes in this chapter. See Recipe Variation sidebar for a recipe for Dill Relish. *Yield: 8 half-pint jars*

What You Will Need

4–5 medium pickling cucumbers

1 green pepper

1 red sweet pepper

3 medium onions

¼ cup canning salt

Ice

Colander

3½ cups white sugar

2 cups cider vinegar

1 tablespoon celery seed

1 tablespoon mustard seed

8 clean, hot half-pint jars and lids

Water-bath canner

SWEET PICKLE RELISH

Wash cucumbers; don't peel. Chop into small pieces. Wash peppers, remove seeds, and chop into small pieces. Peel and chop onions.

Place vegetables in a bowl. Toss with salt. Cover with ice. Refrigerate 2 hours.

Drain vegetables in colander; press to remove water. Combine sugar, vinegar, and spices. Bring to a boil; add vegetables. Simmer 10 minutes.

Pack into jars to ½ inch from rim. Remove bubbles, wipe rims, place lids, and process.

Water-Bath Canner Processing Times for Half-Pints				
Altitude in Feet	0-1,000	1,001-3,000	3,001-6,000	6,001+
Processing Time	10 minutes	15 minutes	15 minutes	20 minutes

Recipe Variation

Dill Relish: To make a dill-flavored relish, use 6 cups chopped cucumbers; 1 cup each chopped red and green pepper; 1 cup chopped onion; 3 garlic gloves, minced; 3 cups white vinegar; ½ cup canning salt; 1 cup sugar; 2 teaspoons each dill seed, celery seed, and mustard seed; and ½ teaspoon turmeric. Follow the recipe for and process like sweet relish. *Yield: 10 half-pint jars*

DRAINING VEGETABLES

Finely chop the vegetables; a food processor can help with this.

Then mix the vegetables with salt, cover with ice, and chill to crisp them.

Pour the vegetables in a colander and let the ice water drain. Press lightly on the vegetables to remove more water.

After the syrup is boiling, reduce heat to simmering and gently slide the vegetables into the pot.

FILLING THE JARS

The sugar and cooking will make a slightly thickened gel around the relish pieces.

If the relish seems watery, use a slotted spoon to remove the pieces from the pan to fill the jars.

Then use just enough fluid from the pan to cover the relish.

Maintain ½-inch headspace in the jar. Make sure to use a bubble stick to settle the relish and remove air.

CORN & PEPPER RELISH

GREAT FOR PICNICS AND SUMMER MEALS

This tangy treat is good in the summer as a cold relish, and some people like it heated in winter for a warm side dish. It makes an excellent accompaniment to summer sausage and crackers. Corn relish is an excellent complement to grilled meats and seafood. It also makes some great dips.

If you don't have fresh sweet corn to use, or you want to make some of this treat in the winter, you can use frozen and thawed whole kernel corn. Bring it to room temperature and drain it well before making the relish.

If you like things spicy hot, replace some of the sweet peppers with hot peppers. *Yield: 5 pints*

What You Will Need

14–18 medium ears fresh corn

3 cups cider vinegar

¾ cup firmly packed brown sugar

¾ cup white sugar

1 tablespoon dry mustard

½ cup chopped green peppers

½ cup chopped sweet red peppers

3 cups chopped onions

2 tablespoons canning salt

1 tablespoon celery seeds

¼ teaspoon red pepper

5 clean, hot pint jars with lids

Water-bath canner

CORN AND PEPPER RELISH

Husk corn, remove silk, cut kernels from cobs, and measure 8 cups kernels.

Bring vinegar and sugars to a boil in a large pot; stir to dissolve sugars. Stir in mustard.

Add corn, red and green peppers, onions, and spices to pot. Cover and boil gently 15 minutes.

Ladle corn mixture into jars to ½ inch from top. Remove bubbles, wipe rims, place lids, and process.

Water-Bath Canner Processing Times for Pints				
Altitude in Feet	0-1,000	1,001-3,000	3,001-6,000	6,001+
Processing Time	15 minutes	20 minutes	20 minutes	25 minutes

Corn Relish Dip

Turn corn relish into a delicious party dip. Everyone will ask for the recipe, and it's so easy to make. Combine ½ cup finely diced chives, 1 crumbled chicken stock or bullion cube, 5 tablespoons sour cream, and 1 pint corn relish. Mix well and allow to sit overnight, covered in the refrigerator. Serve with corn chips or toasted bread. *Yield: 2 cups of dip*

PREPARING THE CORN

White or yellow sweet corn can be used, although yellow corn looks more attractive.

Remove the corn husks and rub the ears with a damp rough cloth to remove silk.

Use a corn cutter or a sharp knife on the ears. To use the knife, hold the cob on a slant and cut away from your body.

Remove kernels at about ¾ their depth on the cob. Do not scrape the cob.

COOKING THE VEGETABLES

Measure all the vegetables after chopping according to the directions.

The mustard is less likely to clump if a small amount of the hot vinegar mix is stirred into it in a bowl, and then this mixture is added to the pot.

Carefully slide all the vegetables into the boiling liquid so it doesn't splash on your hands.

Stir the vegetables frequently so they don't stick to the pan and scorch.

HONEY BARBECUE SAUCE

YOU'LL BE KING OR QUEEN OF THE GRILL WHEN YOU MAKE YOUR OWN SAUCE

You may make great barbecue now, but you'll get rave reviews when you add this special sauce you made yourself. This sauce is great on chicken or ribs. You can use it on the grill or in the oven.

You can start with fresh ripe tomatoes from the garden, or cheat a little and use canned diced tomatoes—yours or commercially canned.

This sauce takes patience and time to make—don't start it the day of the barbecue! But it's worth the time and effort to achieve this wonderful flavor.

After it's made, the sauce is canned or you can freeze it. Make sure to keep opened jars in the refrigerator. *Yield: 4 pints*

What You Will Need

1 large jalapeño pepper
Plastic or rubber gloves
16 cups chopped, peeled, cored tomatoes
1½ cups chopped green peppers
2 cups chopped onions
2 cups chopped celery
Food processor or fine sieve
1¼ cups cider vinegar
1 cup honey
1 tablespoon salt
1 tablespoon paprika
1 teaspoon Tabasco sauce
½ teaspoon garlic powder
½ teaspoon cayenne pepper
4 clean, hot pint jars and lids
Water-bath canner

HONEY BARBECUE SAUCE

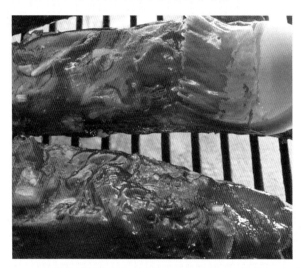

Wearing gloves, wash, core, and chop jalapeño pepper.

Combine chopped tomatoes and remaining vegetables in a large saucepan; simmer until soft. Transfer mixture to a food processor and puree, or push through a fine sieve.

Return vegetables to pot and add remaining ingredients. Bring to a boil, then simmer until thick, about 2 hours, stirring frequently.

Pour into jars to ½ inch from rim, wipe rims, place lids, and process.

Water-Bath Canner Processing Times for Pints				
Altitude in Feet	0-1,000	1,001-3,000	3,001-6,000	6,001+
Processing Time	20 minutes	25 minutes	30 minutes	35 minutes

PREPARING THE VEGETABLES

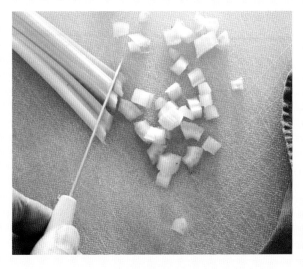

Use gloves to clean hot peppers and remove the seeds before chopping.

When chopping the tomatoes, remove as many seeds as you can. Paste-type tomatoes make the sauce thicker.

All the vegetables in this recipe should be chopped very small so they will cook quickly.

A food chopper or processor will help you quickly chop the vegetables. Do each vegetable separately and measure accurately after chopping.

SLOW COOKING THE SAUCE

The first cooking is to soften the vegetables before you puree them. Don't add water to the pot.

The pureed vegetables will be thin. Add the spices to the puree in the pot at this time.

It takes a long time to thicken the sauce. Cook on low heat and don't cover the pot, as you want water to evaporate.

Stir the sauce frequently early in the cooking and almost constantly near the end to prevent scorching.

OLD-FASHIONED WEINER RELISH

MAKE HOT DOGS THE STAR OF YOUR NEXT PICNIC WITH THIS UNUSUAL RELISH

Tomatoes and peaches seem to be an unlikely combination, but they meld beautifully in this old-fashioned relish recipe. It's colorful as well as tasty and could be a hit at the family reunion picnic.

Relishes traditionally contain small amounts of various fruits and vegetables blended together. Many relishes, like this one, don't contain any cucumbers.

The peaches used in this recipe should be ripe but not soft. Using firm tomatoes such as paste types will make the sauce thicker.

What You Will Need

10 cups peeled, cored, chopped tomatoes
5 cups peeled and chopped peaches
2½ cups chopped onions
1 cup chopped sweet red pepper
1½ cup vinegar
1½ cups honey
1 tablespoon salt
1 teaspoon powdered red pepper
1 teaspoon mustard seed
1 teaspoon cinnamon
½ teaspoon ginger
½ teaspoon cloves
½ teaspoon allspice
12 clean, hot half-pint
Water-bath canner

OLD-FASHIONED WEINER RELISH

Combine chopped tomatoes, peaches, onions, and red peppers in a large pot.

Add vinegar, honey, salt, ground red pepper, mustard seed, cinnamon, ginger, cloves, and allspice to pot.

Bring mixture to a boil and turn it down to a simmer. Simmer the mixture, uncovered, for 2 hours or until it is very thick, stirring frequently.

Pour sauce into jars to ½ inch from the rim. Remove bubbles, wipe rims, place lids, and process.

This relish is traditionally used as a condiment on hot dogs and sausage but would make an excellent addition to pasta salads. It can also be made into a dip. *Yield: 12 half-pint jars*

Water-Bath Canner Processing Times for Half-Pints				
Altitude in Feet	0-1,000	1,001-3,000	3,001-6,000	6,001+
Processing Time	10 minutes	15 minutes	15 minutes	20 minutes

Recipe Variation

If you don't have peaches, plums, apricots, or pears can be substituted. Green peppers can be substituted for red, or you can use half green. You can replace the honey with 2 cups white or brown sugar, but the flavor will be slightly different. You can leave out the salt and change the seasonings to suit your taste. Don't use artificial sweeteners or reduce the amount of vinegar.

PREPARING THE VEGETABLES

The peaches and tomatoes should be dipped in boiling water and then in cold water to remove their skins before chopping. The skins should slip right off.

Remove as many seeds from the tomatoes and peppers as you can when you chop them.

The produce should be diced, but you want the pieces to be recognizable, so don't cut them too fine.

After you have diced the produce, measure it carefully for the recipe.

IS IT READY?

The trick to many relishes is to cook them down to a thickened state without making them into a paste—or burning them.

Cook the relish at a simmer. Stir often but try not to mash the pieces of produce.

It can take 2 hours or longer to cook and thicken the relish. Don't cover the pot.

When the relish is thick—with a clear, shiny gel around the pieces—and it mounds in a spoon, it is finished.

CANNED CHICKEN

CANNED CHICKEN IS TENDER AND READY TO USE IN A WIDE VARIETY OF DISHES

Before freezers became common in kitchens, many meats were canned. Canned meat is totally cooked and has a softer texture than meat that is grilled, fried, or roasted. Your grandmother knew that a tough old hen would become tender during the canning process.

There are hundreds of recipes that use canned chicken, and home-canned chicken can be used in all of them. Canned chicken can be eaten just as it comes from the jar or cooked in other recipes.

You should use only freshly butchered chicken that has been chilled 12 hours (aged) for canning. It's not a good idea to can chicken you buy in the local grocery, as it has often sat for many days. *Yield: Averages 1 quart per chicken*

What You Will Need

1 or more fresh chickens, cleaned and chilled 12 hours

1/2 teaspoon salt per chicken

1/4 teaspoon pepper per chicken

1/4 teaspoon garlic powder per chicken (optional)

1/2 teaspoon dried rosemary per chicken (optional)

2 cups chicken broth per chicken, purchased or homemade

1 hot, clean quart jar with lid

Pressure canner

CANNED CHICKEN

Skin the chicken and trim off excess fat. Cut into quarters.

Place all ingredients in a pot and cover. Simmer until chicken is just a little pink. Remove chicken from pot; refrigerate broth.

Debone the chicken and cut meat into preferred sizes. Remove broth from refrigerator and skim off fat. Return meat to broth and heat to boiling.

Pack hot meat and broth into jars to 1¼ inch from top. Remove bubbles, wipe rim, place lids, and process.

Pressure Canner Processing of Quarts for 90 minutes				
Altitude in Feet	0-2,000	2,001-4,000	4,001-6,000	6,001+
Dial Gauge	11 pounds	12 pounds	13 pounds	14 pounds
Altitude in Feet	0-1,000	1,001+		
Weight Gauge	10 pounds	15 pounds		

Important

See page 158 to learn how to make your own broth. One pint of broth equals 2 cups. Since this recipe uses several spices, try to find an unflavored broth if you purchase it. Don't add salt if you use commercially canned broth, as it is usually very salty. Never add vegetable pieces to broth, as it will change the processing time.

SKIMMING FAT FROM BROTH

DEBONING THE CHICKEN

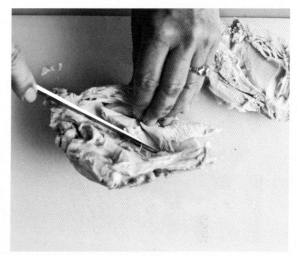

You should remove as much fat as possible from poultry before canning. Excess fat increases the chance of food spoilage.

Remove the skin, which is a large source of fat, and all visible fat while cleaning.

After cooking, remove chicken pieces with a slotted spoon. Put the broth in the refrigerator for an hour or so and fat will collect in a layer on top.

Scoop the soft fat off the broth and discard.

While you are waiting for the fat to separate from the broth, remove the bones from the meat.

Let the poultry cool until you can handle it, then simply pull the meat from the bones with your fingers.

You may want to discard wings and back portions, where little meat can be harvested, or save them to make soup.

At this point the meat should still look a little pink next to the bone and in thicker areas.

CANNED BEEF, PORK OR VENISON

WILD GAME OR TOUGH CUTS ARE BETTER CANNED

Canning lean meat harvested from game animals or meat from older domestic animals is a good way to get a tender, moist product. It will be precooked and ready to eat or use in recipes.

The meat you can should always be fresh, clean meat without any signs of spoilage. Meat should be kept below 40°F until you are ready to can it. Aging meat is not important for its flavor when you can it, and if meat will be sitting for more than two days it is better to freeze it. It can be defrosted and canned later, if necessary.

You can leave the salt out of canned meat or add other spices if desired. *Yield: 1 quart per 2 pounds of meat*

What You Will Need

Beef, pork, or game

Large covered roasting pan

2 cups tomato juice or beef broth per 5 pounds meat

Salt (optional)

1 clean, hot quart jar for every 2 pounds deboned meat

Pressure canner

CANNED BEEF, PORK OR VENISON

Rinse meat, remove bones, and trim off all fat. Cut into pieces that will fit jars, no more than 1-inch thick.

Place meat in roasting pan and add tomato juice or broth. Cover; cook at 350°F until meat is just a little pink inside.

Add ½ teaspoon salt to pint jars or 1 teaspoon to quart jars if using. Fill jars with meat and add hot broth or juice to 1 inch from rim.

Remove bubbles, wipe rims, place lids, and process.

Pressure Canner Processing of Quarts for 90 minutes				
Altitude in Feet	0-2,000	2,001-4,000	4,001-6,000	6,001+
Dial Gauge	11 pounds	12 pounds	13 pounds	14 pounds
Altitude in Feet	0-1,000	1,001+		
Weight Gauge	10 pounds	15 pounds		

A Tip for "Gamey" Meat

For wild-harvested meat you can remove some of the "gamey" taste by soaking the meat in a solution of 4 tablespoons salt to 1 gallon water for 1 to 2 hours before pre-cooking. Rinse meat in clean water before cooking. Cooking the meat in tomato juice will tenderize the meat and help make the flavor milder. Add garlic and black pepper to the tomato juice to improve the flavor.

PRECOOKING MEAT

Meat is always precooked before canning. Cut the meat into strips or chunks that aren't more than 1-inch thick.

Use a covered pan and surround the meat with tomato juice or broth. Plain water can also be used.

Roast the meat at 350°F until a meat thermometer inserted in the thickest meat reads 135°F.

This will mean the meat is pink inside but doesn't leak bloody juice when cut.

CAN ONLY FULL JARS

Weigh drained meat after precooking. It takes 1 quart jar or 2 pints for every 2 pounds of meat.

While you can use both pint and quart jars to can meat, you can't process both at the same time.

Add salt if desired to jars. Pack meat tightly into jars. The broth from precooking is poured over the meat.

Fill jars to 1 inch from the top. Can only full jars; partially full jars are more likely to spoil.

CANNED GROUND MEAT

PRESERVE GROUND MEAT BY CANNING INSTEAD OF FREEZING

When you don't have enough available freezer space for ground meat, try canning it! It will be precooked and ready for your favorite recipes. The texture will be a little softer than fresh ground meat, and it will need to be drained before being used in many recipes.

Can meat as quickly as you can after it is ground; ground meat is an ideal place for bacteria to grow.

You can mix different types of meat in ground meat. Use the leanest meat for canning and drain grease after browning. Fat in meat makes a poor seal and spoilage more likely.

You can grind your own or can ground meat from butchering or purchasing an animal. *Yield: 2 quarts per 3 pounds meat*

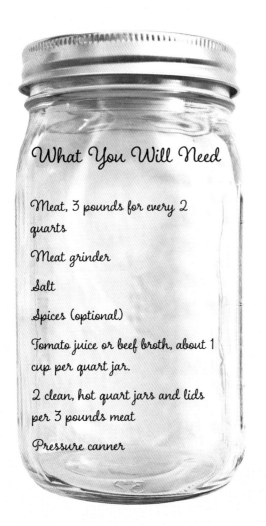

What You Will Need

Meat, 3 pounds for every 2 quarts

Meat grinder

Salt

Spices (optional)

Tomato juice or beef broth, about 1 cup per quart jar.

2 clean, hot quart jars and lids per 3 pounds meat

Pressure canner

CANNED GROUND MEAT

Put meat through meat grinder. Mix in spices, if desired. Do not use sage.

Place meat in a frying pan or saucepan and brown. Drain off excess fat. In a separate pan, bring juice or beef broth to a boil.

Place meat loosely in jars; don't press or pack down. Add a small amount of boiling juice or broth to 1 inch from rim.

Remove bubbles, wipe rims, place lids, and process.

Pressure Canner Processing of Quarts for 90 minutes				
Altitude in Feet	0-2,000	2,001-4,000	4,001-6,000	6,001+
Dial Gauge	11 pounds	12 pounds	13 pounds	14 pounds
Altitude in Feet	0-1,000	1,001+		
Weight Gauge	10 pounds	15 pounds		

GRINDING THE MEAT

If you hunt or raise your own meat, you may want a meat grinder. There are hand-crank and electric models.

Make sure everything is very clean and the meat is good quality and fresh before grinding.

Cut the meat in chunks that are the right size for your grinder, and use something besides your fingers to push the meat through the grinder.

You may want to run the meat through the grinder a second time to mix meats or blend spices.

BROWNING THE MEAT

Place meat in a frying pan and brown until no pink color remains.

Cook meat in small batches so it all browns without burning. Remove any scorched or overcooked pieces.

Drain off excess grease by placing browned meat in a colander and letting grease drip out. Stir occasionally.

Meat can also be put in a colander and gently rinsed with warm water to remove even more grease (this will remove some seasoning, too).

CANNED MINCEMEAT FILLING

USE THIS IN SAVORY PIES OR AS AN UNUSUAL STUFFING FOR POULTRY

Mincemeat is a mixture of meat—sometimes many kinds of meat—fruits, vegetables, and nuts. There are dozens of variations; each culture seems to have its own preferences for mincemeat.

Mincemeat is baked into pies and pastries and used to stuff other meats. It's commonly served at holidays or special occasions.

Older mincemeat recipes often used suet, a hard animal fat. But for healthier arteries, this recipe does not. Older recipes also used lots of spices to disguise less-than-fresh meat that was frequently used in these mixes. For food safety, use only fresh quality meats in your mincemeat, although spices can be used to disguise strongly flavored meats. This recipe can also be made and frozen. *Yield: 7 quarts*

What You Will Need

2 pounds seedless raisins

1 pound dried apricots

3 cups walnuts

Food processor

5 pounds ground meat

2 quarts apple cider, divided

20 cups peeled, cored, and chopped firm apples

5 cups white sugar

2 tablespoons salt

2 tablespoons cinnamon

2 teaspoons ground cloves

2 teaspoons nutmeg

7 clean, hot quart jars with lids

Pressure canner

CANNED MINCEMEAT FILLING

Put raisins, apricots, and walnuts in the food processor; chop coarsely.

In a large pot, combine meat and 2 cups cider; cover and cook until meat is no longer pink. Add apples and remaining cider. Bring to a boil, stir in sugar, and reduce heat when sugar is dissolved.

Add remaining ingredients and simmer until thick, stirring often, about 1 hour.

Fill jars with hot filling to 1 inch from rim. Remove bubbles, wipe rims, top with lids, and process.

Pressure Canner Processing of Quarts for 90 minutes				
Altitude in Feet	0-2,000	2,001-4,000	4,001-6,000	6,001+
Dial Gauge	11 pounds	12 pounds	13 pounds	14 pounds
Altitude in Feet	0-1,000	1,001+		
Weight Gauge	10 pounds	15 pounds		

Recipe Variation

If you prefer really old-fashioned mincemeat, up to 2 pounds chopped suet can be added to this recipe. Suet is dense fat, generally from beef. Ask a butcher for suet and make sure you let him know it's for human use. You can also substitute pears or green tomatoes for the apples; prunes, currants, cherries, or cranberries for raisins or apricots; and other nuts for walnuts.

CHOPPING INGREDIENTS

If you have a food processor or chopper, process each fruit and nut separately for best results. Then combine and mix well.

If no food processor is available, chop dried fruits on a cutting board with a sharp knife.

Put nuts in a plastic bag and pound with a mallet or rolling pin to break.

Make sure the fibrous part of the apple center and seeds are removed before chopping.

THICKENING THE FILLING

Cook the meat in 2 cups of the cider until it is no longer pink. Then add the apples, remaining cider, and sugar.

The sugar and pectin in the apples are the thickeners for the filling. Boil the mixture only until the sugar dissolves.

Reduce heat to simmering as you add the other fruits and nuts. Don't cover the pot.

Stir frequently to keep the mixture from scorching as it thickens. When the mincemeat mounds on a spoon, it is done.

CANNED FISH

CANNED FISH IS SIMILAR TO COMMERCIALLY CANNED TUNA

If someone in your household caught more fish than you can eat, and the freezer is full, can the abundance! It is not recommended that you can small freshwater pan fish, like bluegills, whitefish, or smelt. But larger fatty fish, such as salmon, halibut, mackerel, trout, and steelhead, can reasonably well.

Tuna is hard for homeowners to can; it needs precooking to remove some strong oils, and dark and light meat has to be separated, so it is not recommended in this book.

Fish for canning should have been bled and cleaned immediately and kept chilled until ready to can. If fish cannot be canned the same day it is caught, it should be frozen. Fish can be thawed and then canned. *Yield: About 1 pint per 2 pounds fish*

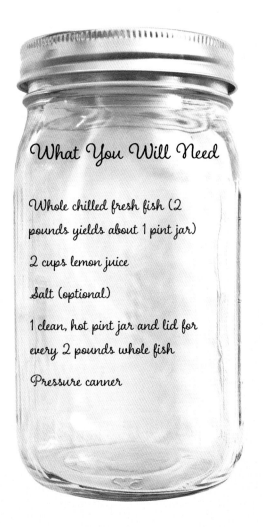

What You Will Need

Whole chilled fresh fish (2 pounds yields about 1 pint jar)

2 cups lemon juice

Salt (optional)

1 clean, hot pint jar and lid for every 2 pounds whole fish

Pressure canner

CANNED FISH

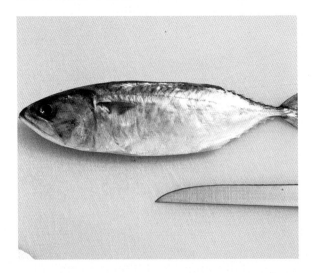

Clean fish and remove head, tail, and fins. Rinse well. Skin and bones may be left. (Remove skin and bones from halibut, however.)

Split fish and slice into chunks about 3½ inches long. Toss fish in lemon juice; drain.

Add 1 teaspoon of salt to each jar, if using; pack fish chunks in jar with skin side out. Do not add fluid. Leave 1 inch space to rim.

Wipe rims, top with lids, and process.

Pressure Canner Processing of Pints for 100 minutes				
Altitude in Feet	0-2,000	2,001-4,000	4,001-6,000	6,001+
Dial Gauge	11 pounds	12 pounds	13 pounds	14 pounds
Altitude in Feet	0-1,000	1,001+		
Weight Gauge	10 pounds	15 pounds		

Important

When salmon and some other ocean fish are canned, struvite crystals occasionally form. These are composed of magnesium ammonium phosphate the fish has absorbed from ocean water. These crystals look like glass but are easy to crush and dissolve in acids, such as a little heated vinegar or the acid in your stomach. They are harmless and safe if eaten. The lemon juice in the recipe may help to avoid this happeneing.

CUTTING UP THE FISH

You can leave some bones in canned fish, as the bones soften during the long processing and become harmless.

If you don't mind small soft bones, just cut the cleaned fish in pieces.

If you want to minimize bones, slide a sharp knife between the ribs and meat and cut off chunks. Use the tail to hold the fish.

Cut the skin off, if desired. For safety, use a filleting glove and sharp knife and cut away from your body.

PACKING THE JARS

Pack chunks of fish tightly into the jars. For a nice look, pack the pieces with skin side out.

The jars will be easier to clean if the skin side is turned in or the fish is skinned.

Add 1 teaspoon of salt to each jar, if desired. For halibut you can add 2 teaspoons of olive oil to keep it more moist.

Don't add any fluid to these jars. Make sure 1 inch of space is left to the rim.

CANNED BROTH OR STOCK

BROTH OR STOCK IS A KITCHEN STAPLE, AND YOU CAN EASILY MAKE YOUR OWN

Broth is invaluable in the kitchen. It's used as the base for soups and stews, for gravy, and for cooking meat to keep it moist. Using broth instead of water makes a good cook shine. You can buy broth, but if you are canning meat, you often have bones and scrap meat that will make excellent broth. You might want to make broth first, to can the meat in it.

Making your own broth allows you to adjust the seasonings and salt in the broth. It's economical, too; you are turning waste into something valuable. After opening jars of broth, freeze the excess or refrigerate and use within three to four days.

This recipe explains how to make the broth as well as can it. *Yield: Roughly half the water added to the pot*

What You Will Need

Fresh meat scraps and bones with meat attached

Bone saw or heavy duty knife

Canning salt

Seasonings (optional; see ideas in sidebar)

Clean, hot quart jars with lids

Pressure canner

CANNED BROTH OR STOCK

Break up or saw large bones. Place bones and meat in a large pot.

Add water to cover bones. Add salt to taste, about 1 teaspoon per quart of water. Add seasonings, if desired. (See Seasoning Tips)

Simmer, covered, for 3 to 4 hours. Remove bones from pot and scrape off any meat into pot. Refrigerate broth 2 hours; skim off fat; discard.

Bring broth back to boiling. You can strain broth or leave small meat pieces in it. Pour into jars; leave 1 inch to rim. Wipe rims, top with lids, and process.

Pressure Canner Processing of Quarts for 25 minutes			
Altitude in Feet	0-2,000	2,001-4,000	4,001-6,000	6,001+
Dial Gauge	11 pounds	12 pounds	13 pounds	14 pounds
Altitude in Feet	0-1,000	1,001+		
Weight Gauge	10 pounds	15 pounds		

Seasoning Tips

Adjust the salt in the broth to your taste or leave it out altogether. Black or red pepper, powdered onion, and garlic are good seasonings for most broth. Don't add whole spices directly to the broth; instead use a spice bag or ball when cooking. Celery seed, celery leaf, or parsley and minced rosemary are excellent for chicken broth. Don't add sage—it turns bitter.

BREAKING UP THE BONES

Bones are cut or broken to expose marrow, which flavors the stock, and to make them fit into the pot.

Large bones may need to be sawed with a butcher's saw. A hacksaw with a clean blade could be used at home.

Knuckle cartilage, necks and tails, rib bones, lower leg pieces, and odd meat scraps are good for broth. Don't use organs for broth.

Bones and scrap meat should be kept refrigerated or frozen until used.

COOKING THE BROTH

Broth should cook long and slow to intensify the flavors. Stir the broth occasionally and break up any large meat pieces.

After 3 to 4 hours of slow cooking, remove bones and scrape any meat pieces off them into the pot.

Pour the broth into a container and chill for several hours. Chilling may make the broth jelly-like. Skim off the fat layer that forms on top and discard.

Break up large pieces of meat and reheat broth to boiling before canning.

STRAWBERRIES & OTHER BERRIES

FREEZE THAT LOCAL HARVEST FOR BERRIES YOU CAN ENJOY ALL WINTER LONG

Freezing is one of the simplest and best ways to preserve fresh berries. Starting with spring strawberries and working your way through fall raspberries gives you a long season of preserving berries. The good news is that you can freeze even a small amount of fruit at a time.

Frozen berries are somewhat softer than fresh when thawed for use, but some whole berries can

What You Will Need

Fresh, ripe berries

Cookie sheets

Freezer bags or containers

STRAWBERRIES AND OTHER BERRIES

Wash strawberries and all other berries, except blueberries. Do not wash blueberries before freezing. They develop tough skins if washed first. Hull or remove stems.

Spread berries in a single layer on a cookie sheet. Place in freezer.

When berries are frozen (after about an hour), remove and pack into bags or containers.

Label and date bags and store in freezer. Wash blueberries before use.

still be used for garnishes. They are excellent for cooking, and you can turn frozen berries into jams and preserves even in the dead of winter, when the hot stove is welcomed.

Select berries at the peak of ripeness for freezing. Never freeze moldy or rotting berries.

TRAY FREEZING

Tray freezing keeps each berry frozen separately and allows you to pack them in a container prefrozen.

Unless they thaw a little and refreeze in a clump, this will allow you to remove some of the contents and keep the rest frozen.

It only takes an hour or so in most freezers for berries to freeze on a tray. You then combine them to save room.

Wash and clean all berries (except blueberries) first. Clean blueberries before using them.

DON'T FORGET TO LABEL

You can probably tell strawberries from blueberries in a clear container, but label anyway.

The label tells you what berries were frozen when and allows you to use the oldest first. Frozen fruits keep up to 1 year.

If you add tray-frozen berries to a container over a period of time, label with the beginning date.

Label containers with the amount of frozen produce, such as 2 cups. This makes using them easy, and you won't defrost more than you need.

SUGAR-PACKED CHERRIES
SUGAR DRAWS OUT THE JUICE AND MAKES A DELIGHTFUL FROZEN PRODUCT

As in canning, there are methods of freezing that work better with certain fruits. Cherries look and taste best thawed when they have been frozen in sugar. The shape and texture remain closer to fresh cherries. If tart cherries are frozen in sugar, they will need less sugar when used in recipes later.

This method is simple and quick. The sugar is added dry but brings out the juice in the cherries and becomes syrup. Do not use artificial sweeteners.

Sweet and tart cherries can be frozen. Pick fully ripened cherries that are free of mold or rot for freezing.

Frozen cherries can be used later to make wonderful desserts and sauces for meats, or they can even be thawed and turned into jelly or pie filling.

What You Will Need

2½ pounds tart cherries for every quart (2 pints) you want to freeze

Cherry pitter (optional but nice)

2 cups white sugar for every quart prepared cherries

Freezer bags or containers

SUGAR-PACKED CHERRIES

Wash cherries; discard unripe, damaged, or moldy fruit. Remove pits with a cherry pitter or cut cherries in half and discard pits.

In a large bowl toss each quart of pitted cherries with 2 cups of sugar. Let stand 20 minutes.

Pack cherries into bags or containers. Don't worry if some of the sugar is still in granular form.

Label and date containers or bags and freeze. Use within 1 year.

Easy Cherry Tarts

Cut circles from prepared pie crust and place in greased tart pans or muffin pans. Push dough firmly into pans and along sides. Bake at 350°F until lightly browned, about 10 minutes. Bring 4 cups of frozen cherries, ½ cup sugar, and 3 tablespoons of minute tapioca to a slow boil: cook 5 minutes. Let cool; fill tart shells and top with whipped cream. *Yield: about 40, 3 inch tarts*

Cherry Benefits

Sweet cherries are good for eating fresh, while tart cherries are good for cooking and making juice. Cherries have more disease-fighting antioxidants than any other fruit. Although adding sugar to them may cancel their weight-loss benefits, cherries have anthocyanins, which relieve inflammation and pain, and melatonin, which helps regulate sleep and mood.

PREPARING THE CHERRIES

Cherries can be frozen with the pits, but most people prefer to start recipes with pitted fruit.

There are hand and electric cherry pitters. Cherry-pitting machines make for much faster cleanup.

To read about how to hand pit cherries, see Cherries in Syrup, page 46.

If it doesn't matter that the cherries look whole, you can simply pull the cherry apart and pick out the pit.

ADDING SUGAR

Cleaned cherries are simply mixed with white sugar, 1 quart of cherries to 2 cups of sugar.

Use a spoon to gently toss the cherries in the sugar. Don't try to crush them.

During the standing time you should find that most of the sugar has dissolved into syrup. Cover containers to keep out insects.

Pack the cherries and syrup into freezer containers. This will freeze into a solid mass, so pack in amounts convenient for use at one time.

PEACH PUREE

SMOOTH, SWEET, AND FULL OF SUNSHINE, PEACH PUREE IS GREAT FOR BAKING OR SAUCES

This recipe takes some precooking, but the wonderful sweet puree is worth it. A puree is fruit that has been softened and then blended into a smooth paste.

Puree is the beginning of many good recipes, including sauces, peach nectar, pastries, and baked goods. Babies love peach puree for dessert.

Peaches are short-season fruits, and when they are abundant in your area, stockpile as many as you can. Look for ripe but firm peaches that are fully colored. Place them on your countertop and cover them with a dish towel for a couple of days. This will finish the ripening and bring out the sweetness of the fruit. Never refrigerate peaches. *Yield: 6 pints*

What You Will Need

4 pounds ripe peaches

1½ cups white sugar

½ cup lemon juice or ½ teaspoon ascorbic acid crystals

Blender or food processor

3 quart-size or 6 pint-size freezer bags or containers

PEACH PUREE

Wash peaches. Dip in boiling water and then in cold water. Slip off skins. Pit and chop.

Bring 2 cups water to a boil; add sugar and stir to dissolve. Add lemon juice or ascorbic acid.

Add peaches to pot. Cook, stirring constantly, 4 minutes; drain. Puree peaches in blender or processor.

Pour puree into bags or containers. Containers with rigid walls need ½-inch headspace for pints, 1 inch for quarts, for expansion. Date, label, and freeze.

REMOVING PEACH SKINS

SOFTENING PEACHES

Peaches are hard to peel unless you blanch them. Get a pot of water boiling and set a pot of cold water near by.

Dip peaches in the hot water on a slotted spoon or skewer them with a long handled fork to dip.

After 60 seconds in hot water plunge the peach in cold water for about 60 seconds.

You may need to cut around the stem area just a bit, but the skin should now slip off easily.

Don't overcook the peaches, or some of the nutrients and flavor will be lost. Make sure they don't stick to the pan.

Drain excess fluid off through a strainer or colander.

If you don't have a blender or food processor, use a potato masher and a wire whisk to blend the peaches smooth, or push peaches through a strainer.

The puree will be lightly sweetened from the sugar and kept from darkening by the lemon juice or ascorbic acid.

SLICED APPLES IN SYRUP

FREEZING APPLES IN SYRUP WITH ASCORBIC ACID MINIMIZES BROWNING AND LOSS OF NUTRIENTS

You probably know that apples will brown when exposed to air, but did you know they even brown when frozen? Cut apples also quickly lose nutrients. Because of this, it's important to freeze apples in syrup.

Choose firm cooking-type apples for freezing, such as Granny Smith, McIntosh, Gala, Rome, or Jonathan, for best results. They should be fully ripe and free of disease or rotted areas.

Thawed apple slices will be softer than fresh apples but still tasty and full of vitamins. Already peeled and sliced, they are a shortcut to fabulous desserts. Use them to make pie fillings, apple cake, and fruit salad. *Yield: About 5 quarts*

What You Will Need

4 cups water

2¾ cups white sugar

2½ teaspoons ascorbic acid crystals

6 pounds fresh apples

5 quart-size containers (best) or freezer bags

SLICED APPLES IN SYRUP

Bring water to a boil; add sugar and let it dissolve. Allow syrup to cool.

Put ¾ cup cool syrup in each container and stir in ½ teaspoon ascorbic acid per container.

Wash, peel, core, and slice each apple directly into containers or bags; press slices down into syrup.

Pour about ¼ cup syrup on top of apples to cover. Leave 1-inch space at top of rigid containers. Freeze.

Important

Each cell of a fruit or vegetable contains water. When that water freezes, it expands and bursts the cell wall. This changes the texture of frozen produce, making it softer when thawed. If you don't plan to cook your frozen items when defrosted, serve them only partially thawed for best appearance. Foods that are mostly water, like tomatoes and spinach, and are not good candidates for freezing.

PREPARING THE APPLES

An apple corer and slicer is an inexpensive tool that makes working with apples easy.

Place the tool over the peeled apple and simply press down to make nice slices. It works like a cookie cutter.

If you don't have a slicer, core the apple with a paring knife and then slice.

Work with each apple next to a container that you have placed some syrup in and drop in the slices so they are covered immediately.

KEEP APPLES UNDER SYRUP

To keep them from darkening and losing nutrients, apples must be kept under the syrup.

As you fill the containers with apple slices, add cool syrup to keep them covered.

Stand freezer bags upright as you fill to maximize coverage and pack them full. After the bags are frozen, they can lay flat.

If using rigid containers, crumble up some waxed or parchment paper and place it between the lid and contents to keep slices under syrup.

MELON BALLS & GRAPES

AN EXCELLENT, LOW-CALORIE DESSERT YOU CAN ENJOY ALL YEAR-ROUND

This combination of fruit, which is generally ripe at the same time, gives you a head start on a low-calorie fruit salad. Since melons and grapes don't hold fresh for long, it gives you a way to preserve a seasonal bounty and enjoy it anytime.

Both of these fruits hold their shape and flavor best when frozen in syrup. Any kind of melon or grape can be used. If buying the fruit, try to think about the colors and how they will look in a mix.

Use fully ripe, sweet, juicy melons and ripe grapes for freezing. Don't cut the melons until you are ready to freeze them. *Yield: About 5 quarts*

What You Will Need

1³/₄ cups white sugar

4 cups water

1 small watermelon

1 medium cantaloupe

1 medium honeydew melon

Mellon baller

10 pounds grapes, half red, half green (seedless are best)

Plastic food wrap

3 sheets clean, white stiff paper

5 quart-size or 10 pint-size containers (rigid containers work best)

MELON BALLS AND GRAPES

Bring sugar and water to a boil; stir to dissolve sugar. Cool to room temperature.

Scrub outside of melons, cut open, remove seeds, and make into melon balls using a melon baller.

Wash grapes; if grapes are not seedless, cut in half, and remove seeds.

Pour about ½ cup syrup in each container. Divide melon balls and grapes among containers, pressing into syrup. Cover with more syrup to 1 inch from top. Weigh down fruit. Freeze.

MAKING THE BALLS

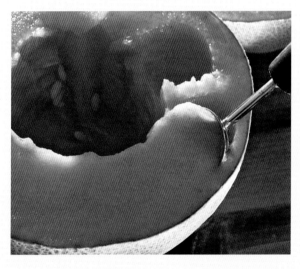

Melons can be cut into chunks, but balls look better. Make balls ½ to 1 inch in diameter for freezing.

A melon baller looks like a deep round spoon. There's a hole in the bottom to let juices out.

Cut the melon and remove seeds. Stick the baller in the melon flesh. Rotate the tool 360° in a smooth, continuous movement.

Deposit balls right into syrup. Be careful not to get into the white area between the rind and flesh.

WEIGHING DOWN THE FRUIT

Fruit often floats up out of the syrup and must be weighed down until frozen to preserve color, texture, and nutrients.

In rigid containers some space must be left at the top for expansion of the food.

To keep fruit under the syrup, fill to 1 inch from rim, then put a piece of plastic wrap or parchment paper on top of the fruit.

Crumble a piece of parchment or other stiff, clean paper and place between the flat piece of paper and lid.

TROPICAL FRUIT BLEND

IF YOU ARE LUCKY ENOUGH TO HAVE AN ABUNDANCE OF CITRUS FRUIT, TRY THIS BLEND

Those who live in warmer climates, or who have relatives who do, may experience times when tropical fruits are abundant. Even in colder areas there may be times when tropical fruits are a good bargain. You can take that abundance and freeze it for times when fresh fruit may not be so readily available.

Unless you live in Hawaii, pineapple is probably not locally grown. But pineapple adds a lot to this recipe, so it is included.

Oranges and tangerines taste better when combined with grapefruit. Seeking out red grapefruit or blood oranges will give you a colorful blend.

Freezer-safe glass containers are best to use with citrus mixes. *Yield: About 4 quarts*

What You Will Need

16–24 oranges, grapefruit, or tangerines

2 whole lemons or limes

2 pounds red grapes

2 ripe pineapples

6 cups pineapple or orange juice, sweetened or unsweetened

4 quart-size or 8 pint-size containers (freezer-safe glass containers work best with citrus)

TROPICAL FRUIT BLEND

Wash and peel oranges, tangerines, or grapefruit. Divide into sections and remove all white membrane. Remove seeds. Slice large grapefruit in half.

Wash lemons or limes. Do not peel. Slice into thin rounds. Wash grapes. Peel and core pineapple and cut into 1-inch chunks.

Fill containers halfway using a mixture of fruit. Place slices of lemon or lime against jar sides, divided among jars.

Continue filling with fruit. Pour juice over fruit to 1 inch from top. Freeze.

REMOVE WHITE MEMBRANE

PREPARING THE PINEAPPLE

For fruit salad mixes you want to remove the tough membrane around each citrus section.

Peel and section the fruit. Using a sharp thin-bladed knife, make a cut on the bottom of the section through both sides of the membrane.

Then make a cut across the fleshy upper side, following the curve of the section.

Grasp the membrane at the bottom of the section and pull it off. Discard seeds and membrane. Large grapefruit sections can be cut in half.

Some stores will peel and core a pineapple, or you can purchase inexpensive tools to do it yourself.

Otherwise, use a sharp knife to cut off the top and a base slice. Slice off the peel. Use the knife tip to dig out any embedded eyes.

Cut the pineapple in quarters. The lighter-colored hard fibrous core should be visible on one edge of each quarter.

Stand the quarter up and slice downward between the core and the flesh. Chop pineapple in pieces.

CORN ON THE COB

HAVE SCRUMPTIOUS, LOCALLY GROWN CORN ON THE COB ALL YEAR-ROUND

Frozen corn on the cob can never match the taste of homegrown corn picked and cooked within minutes of being picked. But properly done, frozen corn on the cob will give you some summer eating in the winter.

Use only fresh, tender corn for freezing. Don't use corn that has sat around in a store for several days or corn that has matured to the doughy stage. Grow the corn or buy it locally, picked the same day. You can freeze just a few ears at a time to keep up with a bountiful home harvest.

Corn must be blanched and quickly cooled before freezing. Quick cooling is the key to keeping frozen corn from having a green or "cob" taste. Steam or boil corn for 3 to 5 minutes before eating.

What You Will Need

Fresh corn in husks

Boiling water in large pot

Ice water in large pot

Freezer containers or bags

CORN ON THE COB

Husk corn and remove silk. Cut ears to fit your containers. Remove undeveloped tips and bad spots.

Place corn in boiling water. Boil 7 minutes for small ears (1¼-inch diameter), 9 minutes for medium (1½-inch diameter), and 11 minutes for large (1¾-inch diameter up). Do not overcook.

With tongs, place ears in ice water for as long as you boiled them. Add ice as needed.

Drain corn, pat dry with paper towels, and pack into containers. Freeze.

BLANCHING TIME VARIES

Blanching stops the action of enzymes in corn and preserves flavor, color, and nutrients.

If you are not good at estimating sizes, measure the diameter (distance across) of your ears at the widest point.

The amount of time to blanch varies by size. Overcooking or undercooking will cause corn to taste funny.

Start counting the blanching time when the pot of water resumes boiling after you've add the corn.

COOL DOWN IS IMPORTANT

Cooling is as important as blanching. Corn that is not quickly cooled may have a green or cob taste when defrosted.

Use ice in your cold dip and replenish as necessary. Work with small quantities of corn at a time.

After the cold dip, cobs can be dried and put on cookie sheets in the freezer until you are ready to bag them.

Don't leave the corn soaking in the cold water too long. It may lose flavor and texture.

GRATED ZUCCHINI

WANT A NICE LOAF OF ZUCCHINI BREAD THIS WINTER?

Even the brownest thumb can probably grow zucchini. And unless you have a large family who really enjoys eating zucchini at every meal, just one or two zucchini plants will give you plenty to eat and have you looking for ways to use the rest.

All kinds of recipes have been devised to deal with excess zucchini. Most of them call for the zucchini to be grated or chopped. Freezing some grated zucchini will allow you to try those recipes in the winter, when a loaf of zucchini bread or a zucchini casserole won't spark a protest from family members.

Zucchini comes in the familiar green color and long shape, but it also comes in yellow or white and in a round shape.

What You Will Need

Young, tender zucchini, about 1 pound per pint container

Grater or food processor

Metal colander

Boiling water

Ice water

Containers for freezing that seal tightly (pint size is generally best)

GRATED ZUCCHINI

Choose young, thin-skinned zucchini. Wash them thoroughly. Grate zucchini into fine shreds using a hand grater or food processor.

Using enough zucchini to fill one container at a time, fill colander and dip into boiling water until translucent, less than 2 minutes.

Drain zucchini, measure the amount, pack into container, leave ¼-inch space to top, and seal. Label container with amount and date.

Sit containers in ice water 10 minutes. Do not get water inside. Wipe containers dry and freeze.

Zucchini Bread

Blend 3 eggs with 2¼ cups sugar. Mix in 2 teaspoons vanilla and 1 cup oil. Blend in 1 teaspoon each salt, cinnamon, baking soda, and baking powder and 3 cups flour. Add 2 cups thawed, drained shredded zucchini, 1 cup crushed pineapple, 1 cup shredded coconut, and ½ cup chopped pecans. Mix well. Bake in greased loaf pan at 350°F for 1 hour. *Yield: 1 loaf*

Baby Zucchini

Zucchini is edible from almost the minute its flower gets pollinated. The tiny fruit is attached to the flower before it opens and only needs a few days to develop to small eating size. Technically zucchini can be eaten at any stage, but huge overgrown zucchini get tough and tasteless. The best zucchini is young and small in size, no bigger around than a 16-ounce soda bottle.

PREPARING ZUCCHINI

Wash zucchini and cut in half or chunks. A food processor can coarsely chop or shred zucchini.

You can use a hand grater or a mandoline to make shreds.

The zucchini can also be chopped with a sharp knife. Pieces should be less than ¼-inch thick.

A pint jar holds about 2 cups of shredded zucchini, which is the average amount used in a recipe.

COOLING THE CONTAINERS

The zucchini must be blanched to stop enzyme action that causes off flavors and loss of nutrients.

Dip small amounts of zucchini in a colander into boiling water until it turns from white to nearly clear.

Immediately pack the hot shreds into containers. The containers must immediately be placed into ice water to stop the cooking.

Be careful not to get water into the containers. After 10 minutes, dry containers and move them to the freezer.

BASIL PESTO

FREEZING PESTO ALLOWS YOU TO PRESERVE HERBS THAT OTHERWISE DON'T FREEZE WELL

Many herbs grown fresh in gardens really don't freeze well and may lose flavor if dried. Basil, cilantro, parsley, and mints are a few. You can, however, preserve these herbs in oil and then freeze them.

Basil is a tender annual plant that is easily grown in the garden. One well-grown plant will provide plenty of leaves. Choose fresh green basil meant for culinary use.

Basil is often used in dishes with tomatoes and peppers. It's also a common ingredient in pasta recipes and vegetable soups. When fresh basil isn't available, substitute a small amount of frozen basil pesto.

Yield: About 12 cubes

What You Will Need

2 cups basil leaves, packed

½ cup salted cashews

2 garlic cloves

Food processor

¼ teaspoon black pepper

½ cup grated Parmesan cheese

½ cup extra-virgin olive oil

Ice-cube tray, metal or plastic, with dividers

Plastic wrap

Gallon-size freezer bag

BASIL PESTO

Wash basil leaves and pat dry. Remove thick stems. Chop finely.

Place nuts and garlic in processor, chop finely, add pepper and cheese, and blend briefly.

Add basil and pour in oil in a thin stream as you blend in short pulses. Do not blend smooth, just mix well.

Pour pesto into metal trays lined with plastic wrap and add dividers; or, pour into divided plastic trays. Freeze. Once frozen, remove cubes and wrap tightly in plastic wrap; store in freezer bag in freezer.

Pesto Facts

Pesto is a sauce that originated in the Mediterranean region and is often part of Italian meals. It gets its name from the fact that originally the nuts and basil were ground together with a mortar and pestle. Pesto is commonly made with basil, but other herbs, such as parsley, can be used. Pine nuts are the traditional nut used with pesto, but modern recipes often use other nuts.

Asian Pesto

Heat 1 cup peanut oil until hot. Turn off heat, add ½ cup peanuts, brown. Save oil. Chop nuts with ¾ cup chopped green chiles, 1 tablespoon chopped ginger, and 4 garlic cloves. Mince 1½ cups basil, ¼ cup mint, and ¼ cup cilantro; add to nuts. Blend 1 teaspoon sugar, 1½ teaspoons salt, and 3 tablespoons lemon juice. Add saved oil to nut mix, stirring constantly.

BLENDING WITH CARE

A blender is suggested for this recipe, but the mixture can also be blended by hand.

Pour a small, thin stream of oil into the basil as you pulse (start and stop) the blender.

If mixing by hand, add a little oil at a time and mash the mix with a pestle or mallet instead of stirring it.

Pesto should not be blended until it is entirely smooth; it should look a little chunky, but the oil should be blended in.

FREEZING IN SERVING SIZES

You could just pour the pesto into a freezer container and freeze. However, it's easier to use when frozen in serving sizes.

Use plastic wrap or parchment paper to line an ice cube or other small tray that has removable dividers.

After filling and smoothing the tray, put in the divider or score the pesto with a knife once it is partially frozen.

After they freeze, the cubes can be placed in another container. Each ice cube portion is about 2 tablespoons of pesto.

GREEN BEANS

EASY TO GROW, EASY TO FREEZE, EASY TO EAT!

There is a recipe for canned green beans in this book, but many people prefer the taste of frozen green beans because they are a bit more crunchy. Frozen green beans need additional cooking before you can eat them. Cook them like you would fresh beans for a taste like fresh garden beans.

Freezing allows you to preserve small amounts of green beans at a time, perhaps when the garden produces more than you can eat at one meal.

Green beans for freezing should be small, fresh, and crisp. Older, larger beans may become tough when frozen. Beans can be cut, left whole, or "frenched" (sliced into small strips).

Freeze your beans in portion sizes that would normally feed your family. If needed, freeze small amounts as they become available on trays and then combine them into containers.

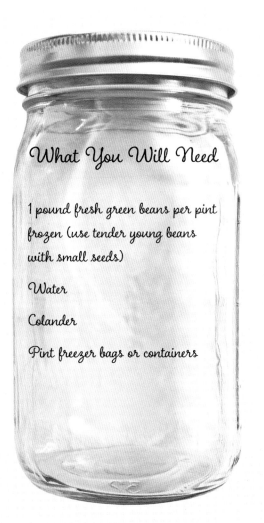

What You Will Need

1 pound fresh green beans per pint frozen (use tender young beans with small seeds)

Water

Colander

Pint freezer bags or containers

GREEN BEANS

Wash beans. Trim off both tips and cut or break beans into 3- to 4-inch pieces.

Bring a pot of water to a boil. Fill colander with beans, lower into boiling water, and boil 3 minutes.

Place colander of beans into a pot of cold water. Leave 5 minutes; drain.

Pack beans into freezer containers. Leave ½-inch head-space at the top of rigid containers. Freeze.

All About Green Beans

Green beans have edible, tasty pods if they are eaten when the seeds inside are still small. There are several shades of green, as well as purple, yellow, and mottled pods. Green beans are low in calories and high in vitamins A, C, and K. They are a good source of fiber, potassium, folate, iron, and magnesium. Green beans are also a good source of riboflavin.

CLEANING BEANS

Store beans without washing them in the crisper bin of the refrigerator. Wash them just before use.

Pick over the beans and discard ones that are limp or brown or have seeds that are too large.

Trim off both pointed tips of each bean. Then break or cut beans into pieces.

If your beans are an older type with a "string" (fiber) along the pod seam, pull that string off with your fingers.

BLANCHING BEANS

Blanching green beans preserves their nutrients, taste, and color.

Don't overcook the beans in the boiling water. Start timing as soon as the water returns to a boil after you've added the beans.

Cooling the beans quickly produces the best-flavored beans. Add ice to the water to keep it cool.

Drain the beans and spread them out on a tray so they can air-dry briefly before you package them. This will keep them from freezing together in a clump.

BROCCOLI

LET THE KIDS HELP FREEZE BROCCOLI, AND MAYBE THEY WILL EAT IT

Some kids do like broccoli. But if yours don't, you may get them to eat it if they help you prepare and freeze it. Freezing is friendlier to little ones than canning, although an adult should always handle the blanching process.

Broccoli is another crop that people often plant more of than they can eat fresh, so freezing the excess is a smart move.

Eat the older, larger stalks fresh and save the young, small florets for freezing. Freeze them soon after picking or bringing home from the store for best results.

Your frozen broccoli will be suitable for any cooked broccoli recipe, but it will be a little soft to serve raw.

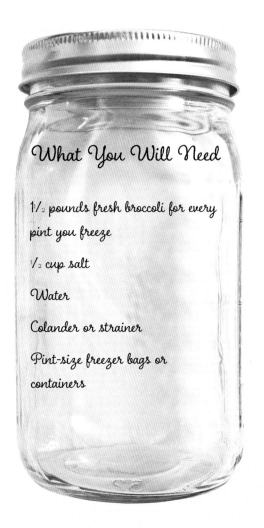

What You Will Need

1½ pounds fresh broccoli for every pint you freeze

½ cup salt

Water

Colander or strainer

Pint-size freezer bags or containers

BROCCOLI

Wash broccoli and trim off heavy stems. Break florets off and split in half to make pieces no more than 1½ inches thick.

Place salt and 1 gallon cold water in a large pot. Add broccoli, leave 10 minutes, and drain.

Place broccoli in colander or strainer and lower into boiling water for 3 minutes. Remove and place in cold water for 5 minutes; drain.

Pack broccoli into bags or containers, filling to the top. Freeze.

Kids' Broccoli Soup

Place 3 cups thawed and drained broccoli, 1 8-ounce jar Cheez Whiz, 1 can condensed cream of celery soup, 2 cups light cream or half-and-half, ¼ teaspoon salt, and ¼ teaspoon white pepper in a slow cooker. You can also add 1 onion, thinly sliced, if the kids like onions. Cook about 3 hours, until broccoli is soft. Blend until smooth. *Yield: About 6 1-cup servings*

Recipe Variation

Brussels sprouts, cauliflower, and asparagus can also be frozen. Sort brussels sprouts into small, medium, and large heads. Blanch small heads 3 minutes, medium 4, and large 5. Break cauliflower into pieces, about 1 inch across. Blanch with 4 teaspoons salt per gallon of water for 3 minutes. Trim scales and tough stems off asparagus, blanch 3 minutes. Freeze as below.

INSECT SOAK

Trim off any tough stems or discolored florets. Break broccoli into small pieces.

Broccoli florets often contain hidden insects. To dislodge them, soak florets in solution of ½ cup salt to 1 gallon cold water for 10 minutes.

Drain and rinse florets well. Blanch in a colander or strainer to preserve color and nutrients.

Cool broccoli quickly for best taste. Add ice to the cooling water and replenish as needed.

TOTALLY FILL CONTAINERS

Drain cooled broccoli and allow to air-dry for a few minutes. Dry florets are less likely to freeze in large clumps.

Florets do not expand when frozen, so pack bags or containers as full as possible.

Don't use containers larger than ½ gallon for original freezing of food. Interior pieces may not freeze fast enough for quality taste.

Smaller packages can be combined into larger bags after they are frozen.

HOMEMADE FRENCH FRIES

QUICK AND EASY FRIES WHEN YOU WANT THEM

White or Irish potatoes do not freeze well in most forms, but you can freeze partially cooked fries so they are quick and convenient to finish cooking later.

If you grow lots of potatoes or can purchase them cheaply, freezing your own fries will save you money over buying them in the store.

There is time invested in peeling the spuds, but you can skip that part if you use thin-skinned potatoes and clean them well. If you make your own fries from fresh potatoes, make extra each time and freeze them.

Potatoes that have been stored for at least 30 days make better fried potatoes. These potatoes can finish cooking in the oven before eating. *Yield: 1 quart bag frozen fries per 3 pounds fresh potatoes.*

What You Will Need

3 pounds medium potatoes for every quart-size bag of fries (potatoes should be firm and have been stored at least 30 days)

5-6 cups vegetable oil

Deep fryer or large pot with metal strainer

Paper towels

Cookie sheets

Freezer containers

HOMEMADE FRENCH FRIES

Scrub potatoes thoroughly. Remove sprouts, green areas, or soft spots. Peel if desired.

Cut potatoes into desired shapes no more than ⅜-inch thick. Rinse in cold water and pat dry with paper towels.

Heat oil to 360°F; add potatoes in batches in fry basket or strainer. Fry until tender, but not brown, about 5 minutes. Drain on towels.

Spread potatoes on cookie sheets and freeze. When firmly frozen, after about an hour, pack into freezer bags and return to freezer.

SHAPING YOUR FRIES

THE FRYING PROCESS

You can cut your fries in a number of ways: straight and skinny, thick and straight, wedges, crinkle cuts, waffles, or plain rounds.

Try to keep all the potatoes fried in one batch the same thickness so they cook evenly.

Leave the skin on to increase the fiber and nutrient content of the potato.

Don't cut too many potatoes at one time, as they will darken as they sit in the air.

Cut potatoes rinsed in cold water have less surface starch and fry better, but make sure they are dry before putting in hot grease.

Use a basket to dip potatoes in hot oil. Don't overload the fryer; fries should be in a single layer.

Preheat oil to 360°F. Potatoes should float and bubble at the sides when dropped in the oil. Don't overcook. The fries should be barely golden.

Bake frozen fries at 400°F for about 20 minutes or deep fry until deep golden before eating.

POULTRY

Whether you grow your own or purchase the specials at the grocery store, frozen poultry should be a staple in your home. Chicken cut in pieces defrosts and cooks quickly; deboned chicken does so even faster. Recipes using chicken are innumerable and range from easy to gourmet.

All types of poultry should be cleaned, chilled, and fresh before freezing. Freezing does not improve poultry that is old and tough or spoiled.

Package chicken according to the way your family likes to eat it. Turkey, goose, and duck are generally frozen whole. Chicken can be frozen whole, as a whole cut-up bird, or sorted into parts—breast, legs, and so on.

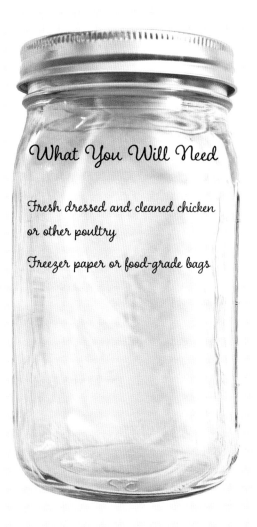

What You Will Need

Fresh dressed and cleaned chicken or other poultry

Freezer paper or food-grade bags

POULTRY

Rinse poultry under cold running water. Rinse body cavity; remove giblets if present. Dry with clean paper towels.

Package the poultry whole, or cut it into the pieces you prefer. Sort pieces by type, such as breasts, or by what is wanted for one meal.

Use freezer paper or food-grade plastic bags just large enough to hold the whole bird or pieces for one meal.

Press air out of bags or press paper firmly against poultry, label and date, and freeze. Pieces are good for 9 months, whole birds 1 year.

CUTTING UP POULTRY

Place the bird on a clean surface. Use a sharp heavy knife for cutting.

To separate legs and thighs, cut between the joints, through the cartilage. Pull the thigh away from the body and cut through the hip joint.

Hold wings away from the body and cut through the shoulder joint. Cut through the ribs near the attachment to the spine and remove the back.

Breasts can be split down the middle or left whole. Clean cutting area with hot, soapy water.

DEBONING AND SKINNING

Use a sharp, thin-bladed knife for skinning and deboning.

Insert the tip of the knife under loose skin with sharp edge facing up. Slice through skin and lift off meat.

For breasts, slip the blade into the meat close to the bone and cut away from you. Some meat generally remains on the ribs.

Slice the flesh on thighs down the length of the bone, fold meat back, and remove bone. Other parts are hard to debone.

GROUND MEATS

THE USES FOR GROUND MEAT ARE ENDLESS

Ground meat of various types is easily frozen and becomes the basis for innumerable meals. If you raise your own animals or hunt, ground meat uses up pieces of meat that aren't suitable for whole cuts. If you are a bargain shopper, freeze ground meat when you come upon a good sale.

Always grind and freeze fresh, wholesome meat that has been kept properly chilled. Freezing does not make bad meat safe to eat.

Lean game meat such as venison benefits from the addition of a little fatty meat, such as fatty pork, to make the ground meat moist and flavorful. Don't add too much fat. It isn't healthy and will shrink a lot in cooking.

What You Will Need

Fresh chilled meat

Meat grinder

Freezer bags, freezer paper, or containers

Food scale

GROUND MEATS

Slice meat into strips that will fit into the grinder and are about 2 inches thick.

Adjust the blades to the grind you prefer. Place meat in the grinder and grind; work in batches and keep meat chilled.

Pack the meat into bags or containers with as little airspace as possible or wrap tightly in freezer paper.

Weigh packages and label them with the meat type, weight, and date. Freeze. Use frozen ground meat within 3 months.

HOME GRINDING MEAT

Before beginning, wash the meat grinder in hot, soapy water and rinse. Wash all counter surfaces as well.

Keep waiting meat covered. If you are grinding a lot of meat before packaging, keep the meat chilled.

Grinding meat with a hand-cranked grinder can be hard work. Plan on calling on help or work with small batches.

You may need to grind some meat a second time. This can be a way to mix meats or mix in spices.

PACKING GROUND MEAT

Exclude as much air as possible from packages to avoid freezer burn. Always use freezer bags or paper, never recycled or storage products.

For long-term storage re-package store-wrapped ground meat.

Pack meat tightly into containers or bags. Press bags flat and push out air. If using a vacuum method, follow manufacturer's directions.

Butcher paper can be wrapped tightly around ground meat and taped. Smooth and flatten.

RED MEAT CUTS

A FREEZER FULL OF MEAT, BOUGHT OR RAISED, MAKES SENSE AND SAVES CENTS

Even if you don't raise your own animals or hunt, you can purchase locally grown, humanely raised meat and freeze it. This saves you money, and you get a superior product over store-packaged meat. Locally raised meat is generally sold in halves or quarters. You pay so much per pound based on the meat's hanging weight, which means the animal has been cleaned. The meat costs the same per pound, whether it's steaks or hamburger.

Whether you shoot it, buy it, or raise it, you won't get as many pounds of meat as the animal's hanging weight. There are scraps, fat, and bones to deduct as waste. Your butcher or seller can give you an idea of how many pounds of meat your animal should yield.

What You Will Need

Fresh chilled meat of any type

Butcher paper or freezer bags

Food scales

RED MEAT CUTS

Decide if you want to freeze individual or family servings of meat.

Cut the meat into sizes you prefer, or sort cut meat into desired serving sizes.

Wrap the meat in butcher paper or pack it into freezer bags. Exclude as much air as possible.

Weigh packages and mark weight, type of meat, and date on the package. Freeze. Refer to Chapter 3 for frozen-meat storage times.

If you purchase bulk meat, ask if there is an additional charge for the cutting and packaging. Getting ham, bacon, and sausage made generally costs extra.

MAKE IT EASY

Freezer burn makes meat look dry and whitish. It may affect flavor but the meat is safe to eat. Meat is also safe to eat if it thaws, but still feels cold. Thoroughly cook it first. Meat that only partially thaws can be re-frozen, although some quality is lost.

Important

If your meat is cut, packaged, and frozen at the butchers, you can fill your freezer without harming the motor. But if you butcher your own meat or receive a large amount of fresh meat, you may not be able to freeze it all at once. It's generally safe to freeze only 2 to 3 pounds of food per cubic foot of freezer space at a time. The rest of the meat will need to be refrigerated or put on ice until the first batch is frozen.

WRAPPING MEAT IN PAPER

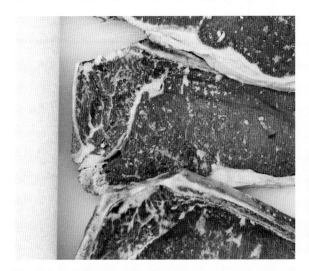

Use only butcher or freezer paper and tape for wrapping meat.

Flat cuts: Center the meat on a sheet of paper. Bring 2 sides up over the meat. Fold a bit of each raw edge under to double the edges.

Fold the paper over the meat, pressing it down against the meat. Repeat with other sides and tape.

Rounded cuts: Center on one corner of the paper and roll the meat in the paper. Then fold over ends and tape.

WEIGHING AND MARKING PACKAGES

Package only the amount of meat you typically use in a meal, such as 2 steaks.

For larger cuts like roasts and hams, weigh the meat after packaging and mark the weight on the package.

Later, this will help you determine how many servings you have in that package.

Make sure you plainly label the package with the type of meat (beef), the cut (sirloin roast), and the date. Use a marker made for freezers.

FISH IN LEMON GLAZE

THIS LIGHT LEMON GLAZE HELPS MAINTAIN GOOD FISH QUALITY

If you catch more fish than you can eat, you can easily freeze it. All kinds of fish, from smelt to shark, can be frozen. For top quality, fish must be cleaned and chilled as quickly as possible and then frozen while fresh. If the fish are large, you may want to fillet them.

Fish are pretreated for freezing with 1 of 2 solutions, depending on whether they are classified as fatty or lean fish. Just as blanching improves the keeping quality of fruits and vegetables before freezing, pretreating gives you the most nutritious and flavorful fish.

If you use the glaze in this recipe, which is good for both types of fish, other pretreatments are not necessary.

What You Will Need

5-10 pounds fresh, cleaned fish, whole or fillets

½ cup lemon juice

3½ cups water

2 packets unflavored gelatin

Freezer paper or bags

FISH IN LEMON GLAZE

Place fish on a tray in the freezer. Chill 10 minutes.

Combine lemon juice and water. Transfer 1½ cups to another bowl and dissolve gelatin in it. Heat the remaining liquid to boiling.

Slowly pour the gelatin mix into the boiling water. Cool mixture to room temperature.

Dip cold fish into gelatin, drain, and place back in freezer; freeze 10 minutes and then repeat dip. Allow fish to freeze firm on surface. Package, weigh, label, and freeze. Keeps up to 6 months.

Clams, oysters, and scallops should be alive until just before freezing. They can be shucked, washed, and packed into freezer containers: leave ½ inch at top or freeze them in the shell. Shrimp can be frozen after cooking, but for long storage, freeze in shell raw, with head removed. For crab, remove back, legs, guts, and gills and boil 5 minutes. Quickly cool, then package for freezing.

Alternative Fish Preservative Dips: For fatty fish (salmon, steelhead, bluefish, tuna, mackerel, trout, mullet), mix 2 tablespoons ascorbic acid (found with canning supplies) to each quart of cold water and immerse fish for 30 seconds. For lean fish (freshwater panfish, smelt, catfish, flounder, cod, grouper, snapper, whiting), mix ¼ cup salt to each quart cold water and immerse fish for 30 seconds.

PREPARING THE GLAZE

Use concentrated commercial lemon juice and unsweetened, unflavored gelatin.

Mix all the lemon juice and water together; mildly warm water works best. Transfer 1½ cups to another bowl. Put the gelatin in this and stir to dissolve.

Bring the rest of the lemon mixture to a boil. Slowly pour the dissolved gelatin into it and turn off heat.

Allow this mixture to cool to room temperature. Make sure the fish are very cold before dipping.

SETTING THE GLAZE

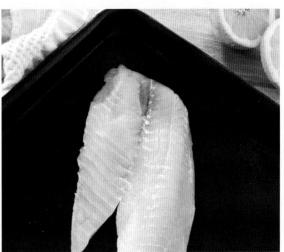

Dip cold fish into the glaze. A thin ice layer should form on the surface.

A piece of parchment paper on the tray will keep the fish from freezing to it. Place fish in freezer.

Freeze 10 minutes; repeat the dip. Spread the fish on the tray so they don't touch. Then let them freeze about 30 minutes.

After they are frozen firm, the fish can be wrapped or placed in freezer bags so they don't stick together.

MILK, CREAM & CHEESE
THESE ITEMS GENERALLY AREN'T FROZEN, BUT IF YOU HAVE AN ABUNDANCE, HERE ARE SOME TIPS

If you have a family cow or goat, there may be times when you have much more milk than you can use. Or if you are a bargain hunter and come upon milk products at a price too low to resist, you may want to freeze some of the excess.

Freezing milk products is not the best way to store them, and they do lose some quality or texture. Even commercial ice cream starts to lose its quality after about a month of storage, especially if opened. But some frozen dairy products will be fine in a pinch and are good for cooking.

Freeze only fresh, clean dairy products. Milk and cream should be pasteurized before freezing.

Dairy Items and Freezing

Butter: Freezes well.

Hard cheese: Will freeze but is crumbly when thawed.

Soft cheese (cottage, cream): Does not freeze well.

Whipped cream: Can be frozen

Heavy cream: Can be frozen if you add ½ cup sugar per quart, then heat it to 170°F for 15 minutes before freezing.

Sour cream: Does not freeze well.

Whole milk: Can be frozen but will separate when thawed.

Buttermilk: Freeze like whole milk.

Homemade yogurt: Will freeze but may taste more acidic when thawed.

FREEZING WHIPPED CREAM

If you have lots of cream, whip some and freeze it for garnishing desserts. Cream will whip after freezing but only to a soft stage.

Whip the cream with about ¼ cup of sugar per quart of milk until stiff peaks form.

Line a tray with parchment paper and put puffs of the whipped cream on it. Place the tray in the freezer.

When the whipped cream dollops are frozen solid, they can be packed into bags or containers.

Simple Rice Pudding

Put one cup of water, 1 cup of sugar, 1 cup of rice, 1 beaten egg, 1 teaspoon vanilla, ½ teaspoon nutmeg, and 1 quart of thawed milk in a large sauce pan. Cook slowly for about an hour, until rice is soft and pudding is thick. Stir in 1–2 cups of raisins. *Yield about 8 servings.*

FREEZING BUTTER

Butter is one of the best dairy items to freeze. It will hold its texture and taste for at least 9 months if packaged properly.

You can freeze commercial sticks or blocks of butter by overwrapping them in freezer bags or freezer paper.

You can also mold butter into forms with butter molds and freeze those. Little patties of butter can be frozen if separated with pieces of parchment paper.

Homemade butter can be pressed into containers and frozen.

FREEZING WHOLE MILK

Freezing milk may not kill disease organisms. Milk should be pasteurized before freezing.

Frozen milk may separate into a watery and a thicker layer when thawed. It can be blended back together and is perfectly safe.

Freeze milk in freezer-safe glass containers for the best flavor. Don't freeze in cardboard cartons.

Leave 1½ inches of space at the top of narrow-mouthed containers, ½ inch for pints, and 1 inch for quarts in wide-mouthed jars. Milk stores about 3 months.

EGGS

YES, YOU CAN FREEZE EXCESS EGGS WITH THIS QUICK AND EASY METHOD!

If you have chickens, even a few, there may be times when you have more eggs than you know what to do with. And there may be times when you don't get many eggs at all. And if you don't have chickens, there are often times of the year when eggs are very inexpensive at farmers' markets and grocery stores. Freezing the excess will let you even out the harvest or take advantage of bargains.

Frozen eggs can be used for baking and scrambled eggs or omelets. They need to be thawed to room temperature before use. You can separate the yolks and whites or freeze whole eggs. Freeze only fresh, quality eggs that have been properly stored. Frozen eggs store about 1 year.

What You Will Need

Fresh eggs

Sugar or salt

Strainer

Ice-cube tray lined with plastic wrap

Freezer bags or containers

EGGS

Make sure eggs are clean and fresh. Break eggs into a container until you have 1 cup of eggs.

Add either 1½ tablespoons sugar or ½ teaspoon salt to each cup of eggs. Blend gently; do not whip in air.

Pour eggs through strainer into another container. Measure 3 tablespoons and pour into each tray compartment. Freeze.

When cubes are frozen, remove from tray and pack in freezer bags or containers. Label the package "sweet" or "salty." Each cube equals 1 egg.

Important

Before breaking eggs, wash them well in lukewarm water with a mild soap. Eggs are porous, and using hot water may open the pores and allow microbes inside the egg. Don't consume or freeze cracked eggs. After thawing frozen eggs, make sure they are thoroughly cooked before eating. Don't consume raw dough or batter with eggs in it. Freezing does not kill all disease organisms.

Before You Freeze Eggs

Grocery stores feature many frozen breakfast entrees with scrambled eggs, but they are flash frozen. It isn't as easy at home. Eggs can be scrambled and frozen, but they may not have the taste and texture of just-cooked eggs. Using milk, cheese, and meat in the eggs like an omelet improves the product. Don't freeze large amounts, and use them quickly. Heat in the microwave for best results.

BLENDING EGGS

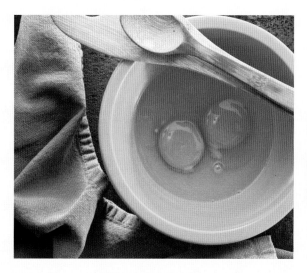

You don't want to blend a lot of air into the eggs. Don't use a whisk or blender; use a spoon or spatula.

Add the sugar or salt and slowly stir the eggs so that the yolks break and blend with the whites.

Pour the eggs through a strainer to further break down solid pieces.

If you don't have ice-cube trays, use a muffin pan sprayed with cooking spray and measure 3 tablespoons of egg mix into each cup.

THAW CUBES BEFORE USE

After they are frozen, the egg cubes should be individually wrapped in plastic wrap and then stored in a container.

Make sure to label your containers of eggs as to whether they have sugar or salt added so you will know what to use them in.

Each egg cube equals 1 large egg.

Remove what cubes are needed and allow them to defrost in the refrigerator before use. Don't use the microwave to defrost egg cubes.

DRIED TOMATOES

DRIED TOMATOES ADD A UNIQUE, GOURMET TASTE TO MANY DISHES

Sun-dried tomatoes are one of those gourmet food items that have worked their way down to ordinary cooks. The salty, tangy, almost smoky flavor of dried tomatoes complements many foods. Mediterranean cooking frequently uses them, probably because the dry sunny climate of that region makes it easier to dry tomatoes.

Sun drying tomatoes isn't easy in other places because tomatoes have a high water content and other places lack hot, dry weather. But it's worth a try if you have an abundance of tomatoes and enjoy the taste. Dried tomatoes are for special recipes and are not the preferred way to preserve your tomato harvest.

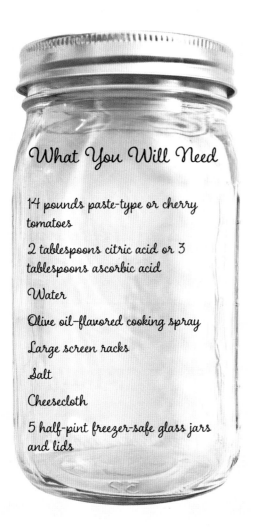

What You Will Need

14 pounds paste-type or cherry tomatoes

2 tablespoons citric acid or 3 tablespoons ascorbic acid

Water

Olive oil–flavored cooking spray

Large screen racks

Salt

Cheesecloth

5 half-pint freezer-safe glass jars and lids

DRIED TOMATOES

Wash tomatoes. Cut small ones in half, larger ones in quarters. Remove seeds, if desired.

Mix citric or ascorbic acid with 2 quarts water. Submerge batches of tomatoes for 10 minutes; drain.

Spray screens with cooking spray. Arrange tomato pieces on screen; be sure they do not touch. Sprinkle lightly with salt. Cover with cheesecloth. Dry until leathery, with no obvious moisture (2 to 3 days).

When dry, pack pieces in jars and store tightly sealed in the freezer.

Choose perfectly ripe tomatoes for this recipe. Cherry tomatoes can be dried in halves or whole.
Yield: 5 half-pint containers

THE SUN-DRYING PROCESS

Screens should be made of food-safe plastic, fiberglass, or stainless steel, never galvanized wire.

Wait until a stretch of hot, dry weather is predicted to begin. Long sunny days are needed; don't wait too late in the season.

Elevate the screens off the ground. Cover the food with cheesecloth or the lightest-spun garden row cover to keep out insects.

If dew is common in your area, move the trays indoors at night. This also protects food from animals.

PROPERLY DRIED TOMATOES

It can take several days for the tomatoes to dry completely.

Starting with meaty, paste-type tomatoes will make drying faster and produce a better product.

Properly dried tomatoes are more rubbery than crisp. They bend rather than snap. They should show no droplets of moisture on the surface.

Store dried tomatoes in tightly sealed containers. Add a bit of powdered milk twisted in cheesecloth to absorb moisture. Refrigerate.

MAKING RAISINS

MAKE YUMMY HONEY-COATED RAISINS FROM EXCESS GRAPES

Commercial raisins are often coated with honey. Honey is a natural preservative as well as a sweetener. The raisins you make in this recipe will taste much like commercial raisins without any other chemical preservatives.

Raisins are great natural snacks, or you can use them in cooking. Grapes have been dried in the sun for thousands of years to make raisins, but they dry quickly and easily in a food dehydrator and are a good starter project for learning food-drying techniques.

Raisins can be made from any grapes, although seedless work best. Light-colored raisins are made from white or green grapes. The grapes should be fully ripe and sweet. *Yield: 3 cups*

What You Will Need

6 pounds grapes, any color (seedless are best)

1½ cups water

½ cup white sugar

½ cup mild, light honey

Food dehydrator

Storage bags or jars to hold about 3 cups raisins

MAKING RAISINS

Wash grapes. If grapes have seeds, cut in half and remove.

Bring water to a boil and stir in sugar to dissolve. Cool to barely warm, add honey, and stir well.

Soak grapes in honey mixture for 5 minutes; drain. Arrange grapes on dehydrator trays.

Follow dehydrator directions for drying. Expect 15 to 20 hours drying time. Store dried grapes in tightly sealed containers.

Use Rice to Absorb Moisture

All food pieces may not get equally dry. Put the dried food in a large glass or plastic container with a tight-fitting lid. Add 1 cup dried white rice and stir or shake the container every day. (If moisture appears on the sides, return food to dehydrator.) The rice and very dry pieces will absorb any remaining moisture. After a few days, remove rice and package for storage.

Recipe Variation

Alternative Pretreatment: Put grapes in a colander and dip into boiling water for 30 seconds and then quickly plunge into ice water; drain. Add 1 teaspoon crystalline ascorbic acid or 6 crushed plain 500-milligram vitamin C tablets (sold as vitamins) for each 2 cups water; stir to dissolve. Cover grapes with water; soak 5 minutes; drain; begin drying process.

THE HONEY DIP

Choose honey that has a light color and mild flavor for this dip. Make sure the sugar water is cool before adding honey.

All honey could be substituted for sugar, but the raisins would have a strong honey flavor.

This recipe makes about 2 cups of honey dip. You may need to double the amount to cover all the grapes.

Let the excess honey dip drip off the grapes before arranging them on dehydrator trays.

STORING RAISINS

Follow the directions for conditioning dried fruit in the Green Light sidebar to make sure raisins are perfectly dry.

Package the raisins in small quantities. If some mold, only that package will need to be discarded.

Use glass or food-grade plastic containers with tight lids for storage. Recycled food containers are fine if they are washed with hot water and soap and dried.

Raisins may also be packaged with vacuum-type food bags. Store all containers out of direct sunlight.

BANANA CHIPS

THIS SNACK IS CRISPY, SWEET, AND NUTRITIOUS

Banana chips are another good beginner's project in food drying. Bananas are available all year-round for experimentation at reasonable prices. And banana chips are delicious, satisfying the sweet tooth as well as offering up some good nutrition.

This recipe uses a juice dip as a pretreatment. You can also use the honey dip described in the recipe Making Raisins (page 198). However, bananas discolor when exposed to air, and the juice dip helps preserve their color better than honey does. Unsweetened pineapple, lemon, or lime juice or a combination of juices could also be used in this recipe.

Banana chips can be eaten as snacks or used in homemade trail mixes, on cereal, and in cooking. Choose ripe but firm bananas. *Yield: 2 cups*

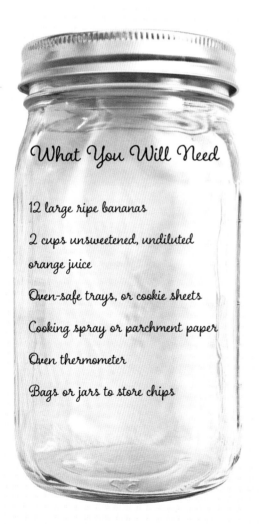

What You Will Need

12 large ripe bananas

2 cups unsweetened, undiluted orange juice

Oven-safe trays, or cookie sheets

Cooking spray or parchment paper

Oven thermometer

Bags or jars to store chips

BANANA CHIPS

Peel bananas. Remove any soft spots. Put orange juice in a bowl. Slice bananas ¼-inch thick directly into juice. Let chips soak 5 minutes.

Coat trays or sheets with cooking spray or line with parchment paper. Drain banana chips and place slices on trays; do not let them touch.

Place trays in oven with thermometer inside. Prop oven door open 1 to 2 inches. Heat to 140°F to 160°F. Rotate trays every 3 to 4 hours. Dry until crisp, about 10 hours. Cool and package in bags or jars.

Delicious Mixes

Mix banana chips with dried cherries, cranberries, apricots, raisins, apples, or nuts. You can also add chocolate, peanut butter, butterscotch, or vanilla chips, or candy-coated chocolates. Small pretzel sticks or dry cereals can be added, as well. For a spicy mix, spread some of the ingredients on a tray and lightly spray with cooking spray. Then toss with packaged dry taco seasoning mix.

THE DIP

Use unsweetened, undiluted pure orange juice for the dip. Pasteurized juice is fine.

The juice acts as a pretreatment and color preserver. Make sure you have enough juice to totally cover the banana slices.

Slice peeled bananas right over the bowl so they don't turn dark when exposed to air. Don't soak longer than 5 minutes.

Let the bananas drain and air-dry well before drying begins. The juice dip is edible.

OVEN-DRYING PROCESS

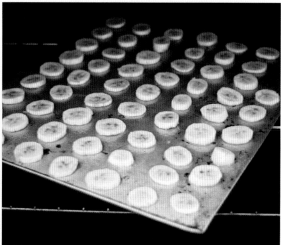

Arrange banana chips on cookie sheets or trays lined with parchment paper or sprayed with cooking spray.

Parchment paper or cooking spray keeps chips from sticking to the trays or sheets as they dry.

Arrange slices so they don't touch. Arrange cookie sheets or trays so there's space between them and between them and the oven walls.

Set the oven at 140°F and prop the door open. To help chips dry evenly, rearrange the sheets every few hours.

DRIED APPLES

DRIED APPLES ARE GOOD FOR SNACKS OR COOKING

Apples store well fresh, but drying them can reduce storage space and make for some pretty tasty eating. They are lightweight but sweet and nutritious snacks for camping and hiking trips. Dried apples are also good cooked in a number of ways. Dried apple pie is an old pioneer favorite.

Choose firm, crisp types of apples, such as Golden Delicious, Granny Smith, McIntosh, or Rome, rather than softer ones for drying. Most people peel their apples before drying, but some choose to dry apples with the peel on.

Dried apples can even be used to make decorative wreaths and potpourri. This recipe calls for the apples to be dried in a dehydrator, but apples are good candidates for sun and oven drying, too. *Yield: 6 cups*

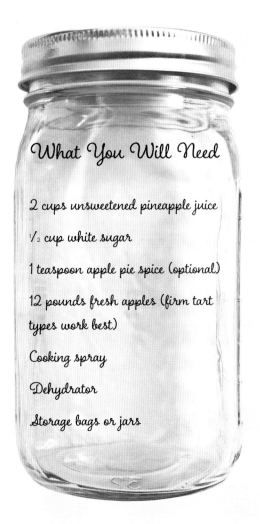

What You Will Need

2 cups unsweetened pineapple juice

½ cup white sugar

1 teaspoon apple pie spice (optional)

12 pounds fresh apples (firm tart types work best)

Cooking spray

Dehydrator

Storage bags or jars

DRIED APPLES

In a saucepan heat pineapple juice, sugar, and spice, if using; stir just until sugar dissolves. Allow to cool.

Wash, peel, core, and quarter apples. Slice quarters into ¼-inch-thick pieces directly into cool juice mix. Soak 10 minutes.

Drain apples well. Coat trays of dehydrator with cooking spray. Make sure slices are not touching.

Dry until leathery, about 12 hours. Pieces should not stick together or show moisture. Cool and package in bags or jars for storage.

Fried Dried Apple Pies

Place 6 cups dried apples, 3 cups water, 1 tablespoon lemon juice, 1 teaspoon cinnamon, ½ teaspoon nutmeg, and 1 cup packed brown sugar in a pot. Simmer until soft. Roll out a prepared piecrust; cut into 6-inch circles. Drain apples and put a spoonful on each. Fold over and crimp. Deep fry at 360°F until brown. *Yield: about 10 fried pies*

MAKE IT EASY

If you are drying apples to make a wreath, leave the peel on and slice apples into thin rounds instead of quarters. It takes a lot of apples to make one wreath. After they are dried, there should be a hole in the center; string them on a wire or cord. Use dried cranberries or cherries, cinnamon sticks, dried flowers, and ribbons to add color to the wreath.

PREPARING THE APPLES

You can buy electric or hand-cranked machines that will peel and core apples for you.

If you peel by hand, at least buy an inexpensive apple corer-slicer to save time.

Try to keep the slices at an even thickness so they dry at the same rate. Thinner pieces dry faster.

Slice apples directly into the pretreatment juice to keep the color from darkening. Make sure the dip is cool. The spice can be omitted from the dip.

TESTING FOR DRYNESS

Apples will normally dry in about 12 hours, but could dry as soon as 6 hours, depending on the machine and other factors.

Check the apples at 6 hours and every hour after. Dried apples are leathery rather than crisp.

Pile a few pieces on top of each other, top sides facing in, and press down with a finger. If the pieces don't stick together, the apples are dry enough.

Cool apples before packaging.

DRIED CHERRIES

DRIED CHERRIES ARE FULL OF NUTRIENTS AND ANTIOXIDANTS

Dried cherries are available in stores but are quite expensive. If you have cherry trees or are near a cherry-growing region where they are sold at farmers' markets, you can dry cherries yourself and save money.

Dried cherries have all the antioxidants and vitamins that fresh cherries have. They add a gourmet touch and sweet, tangy nutrition boost to cookies, candies, and other baked goods.

Tart cherries are best for drying, although you can use sweet cherries, too. Just be sure they are fresh and fully ripe. Cherry-pitting machines are available to help with that time-consuming prep step. See the Cherries in Syrup recipe (page 46) for tips on how to hand pit cherries. *Yield: 3 cups*

What You Will Need

8 pounds tart cherries

Cooking spray

Dehydrator

Storage bags or containers

DRIED CHERRIES

Remove stems from cherries; wash and pit. Cut each cherry in half.

Spray dehydrator trays with cooking spray. Arrange cherry halves on trays so that they do not touch each other.

Dry cherries until raisin-like. This can take up to 36 hours.

Allow cherries to cool; package in bags or containers for storage. Dried cherries need conditioning; see Making Raisins recipe (page 198).

PREPARING CHERRIES

Wash cherries just before you plan to use them. Sort through and remove any soft, moldy, or bird-pecked fruit.

Pit the cherries. You can dry them whole or in halves, so it's fine to pull them apart to get the pit out. Halves dry faster.

Cherries don't need a pretreatment if they are dried in halves.

If you want to dry cherries whole for appearance, pit them and dip in boiling water for 30 seconds before drying.

LETTING CHERRIES COOL

It can take a long time to dry cherries, even in a dehydrator. After 24 hours, check them every hour or so.

Cherries shrink and become raisin-like when dried. The color will get darker.

After removing cherries from the dehydrator, allow them to cool for an hour or so before packaging. Packaging while warm causes condensation.

Condition dried cherries as described in the Making Raisins recipe.

FRUIT LEATHERS

KIDS, BIG AND LITTLE, LOVE FRUIT LEATHER—MAKE YOURS HEALTHY AT HOME

If you worry about what might be in that fruit leather you buy at the store, make your own. Warning: You may never get much fruit leather to store, as it is so good when freshly made, the family will eat it right up.

This recipe makes the fruit leather in the oven, but it can be made in the dehydrator, too. It's a good family activity for cold winter days. This recipe calls for fresh fruit, but thawed frozen fruit or drained, canned fruit can also be used.

Applesauce, yours or commercial, can be used in all fruit leathers to make them sweeter and a bit more pliable when dried. *Yield: 2 trays*

What You Will Need

1 pound fresh apricots

Water

1 quart fresh strawberries

Food processor

½ cup applesauce

½ cup mild-flavored honey

2 13x 15-inch cookie sheets

Plastic wrap or parchment paper

Oven thermometer

FRUIT LEATHERS

Dip apricots in boiling water and then in cold; slip off skins. Remove pits. Wash and hull strawberries.

Process fruit until smooth. Add applesauce and honey; blend to mix.

Line cookie sheets with plastic wrap or parchment paper; smooth out wrinkles. Spread on the puree.

Place in oven, prop open door 1 to 2 inches, and heat to 140°F. Dry until center doesn't dent to touch, about 18 hours. Peel plastic off, cut leather, and cool. Wrap tightly in plastic wrap to store.

POURING THE PUREE

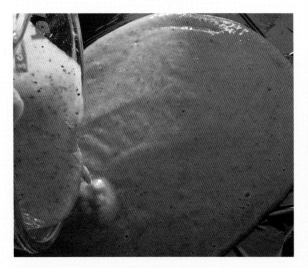

Line cookie sheets with either plastic wrap or parchment paper that has had the wrinkles smoothed out.

Puree should be quite thick. It should be like soft butter, spreadable but not runny.

You need 2 cups puree for each cookie sheet. Don't use too much puree or the leather won't dry correctly.

Spread the puree out to ⅛-inch thickness. It should be even and not touch the sides of the sheet. Leave ¼ inch around the edges.

CUTTING AND ROLLING

To test for doneness, touch the center of the fruit leather. Your finger should not leave a dent. The leather should look shiny.

Cut leather while it is still warm. You can cut it into rectangles or use cookie cutters to cut out shapes.

Rectangles can be rolled around fillings, such as a bit of peanut butter or chocolate.

Wrap each piece of leather tightly with plastic wrap. Store in containers at room temperature for 1 month. Freeze for longer storage.

DRIED POTATOES

WHILE POTATOES STORE WELL FRESH, DRIED POTATOES ARE HANDY FOR CAMPING OR EMERGENCIES

Potatoes can be stored in many ways, but if you want lightweight potatoes for camping and hiking, you may want to dry them. There are now many types of packaged dry potato dishes on the market. You can make your own mixes, and drying potatoes at home allows you to take advantage of the convenience while controlling what goes in the mix.

Long white russet, or "Idaho," potatoes are the best for drying, although any kind can be dried. Potatoes will dry better if they have been in storage for at least a month, but don't use old shriveled and sprouting potatoes. Dried potatoes need to be reconstituted by soaking in water before use, until soft. Then cook like fresh potatoes. *Yield: 4–5 cups*

What You Will Need

Water

1 tablespoon salt (optional)

5 pounds potatoes

Metal colander or strainer

Food dehydrator

Bags or containers for storage

DRIED POTATOES

Bring about 4 quarts water to a boil; add salt, if desired.

Wash potatoes. Peel, if desired, but make sure all green areas are removed. Slice into ¼-inch pieces. Place in colander.

Place colander in boiling water so that all potatoes are submerged; boil 5 minutes. Remove colander from boiling water and dip into cold water for 1 minute.

Drain, place warm potatoes on dehydrator trays and dry until brittle, 8 to 10 hours. Cool and package in bags or containers.

Dried Mix for Scalloped Potatoes

For sauce mix, blend together ½ cup dried milk, 2 tablespoons flour, 2 tablespoons cornstarch, 1 tablespoon onion powder, 1 tablespoon dried minced parsley, ⅛ teaspoon seasoned salt, and ⅛ teaspoon pepper. Store 3 cups dried potatoes and sauce mix in separate bags.

To use at home, soak potatoes in hot water for 10 minutes. Drain and place in a greased pan. Empty sauce mix into a separate saucepan and slowly stir in 2¾ cups boiling water. Add 2 tablespoons butter or margarine. Pour sauce over potatoes and bake at 350°F until tender.

For camping, place 2 to 4 tablespoons oil or shortening in a plastic bag or container for greasing the pan and replace the butter. *Yield: 4 servings*

BLANCHING POTATOES

Before drying, potatoes must be blanched to stop enzyme action and reduce starch level.

Blanching also breaks down cell walls and allows moisture to be pulled out more easily. It prevents darkening during drying, too.

Potatoes darken when cut surfaces are exposed to air. Store them submerged in cool water while waiting to blanch them.

Don't overcook the potatoes; they should not get soft. Plunge them in cold water to stop the cooking process after 5 minutes.

DRYING UNTIL BRITTLE

Potatoes can be cut in a number of ways for drying but should not be more than a ¼-inch thick.

Small nuggets may dry faster than rounds, but these will fall through wire racks.

Near the end of the drying time, watch potatoes carefully. If they start to look brown and scorched, remove at once.

Dry potatoes until they are very hard and look slightly shiny. They should shatter when hit with a hammer.

DRIED PEAS

THESE ARE GOOD FOR SOUPS AND CASSEROLES

Peas don't dry as well on the vine as beans do. They can be frozen or canned but are easy to dry for soups and casseroles. Drying them inside keeps them from falling to the ground before they are fully vine dried or being eaten by animals.

For drying choose pea pods that are still green but have mature peas inside. Use English-type pod peas, not Asian or snow peas. Black-eyed peas are more closely related to beans, but they can be dried this way, too.

Dried peas are excellent for split pea soup and to add to slow cooker meals and stews. They are a good source of protein. *Yield: 2 cups*

What You Will Need

8 pounds peas in pods

Metal colander or strainer

Water

Food dehydrator

Bags or containers for storage

DRIED PEAS

Shell peas. Pick out shriveled or damaged peas. Place in colander.

Bring several quarts of water to a boil. Place colander of peas in boiling water for 3 minutes.

Remove colander and quickly dip in cold water for 1 minute; drain.

Spread peas on dehydrator trays and dry until shriveled and hard, about 10 hours. Cool and package for storage.

Nature will help you dry many types of peas and beans right on the vine. As the seeds inside the pods mature, the pods will start to yellow and dry. Once this happens, the whole plant can be pulled and hung upside down inside a dry room to finish drying. Or you can simply leave the plants in the garden and wait until the beans rattle inside the pods.

If foods dried on the vine or you dried foods outside in the sun on trays, it's wise to pasteurize the food to kill any insect eggs laid on it. You can put the food in freezer bags and freeze for 48 hours, or place the food in a single layer on a tray in the oven and heat to 160°F for 30 minutes. Then cool and package.

SHELLING PEAS

If peas are mature, it isn't hard to shell them. Give the pod a squeeze, and it should pop open. If not, run your thumbnail down the side of the pod.

When the pod is open, use your thumb to push the peas into a bowl.

Wash the peas after shelling and allow them to drain.

Blanch the peas in boiling water for 3 minutes and quickly cool in cold water. Blanching stops loss of color and nutrition during drying.

LABELING DRIED PEAS

After the peas are dried and cool, measure them into storage containers. Peas do not need conditioning like fruit does.

Mark the containers with the amount of peas inside and the date you put them in storage. Dried peas keep up to 1 year.

Alternately, combine peas into one large container and measure as you use them.

Store dried peas where rodents and insects can't get to them. Dry, cool spots out of direct sunlight are best.

DRIED ONIONS

DRIED ONIONS ARE HANDY IN THE KITCHEN, AND YOU WON'T CRY WHEN YOU USE THEM

While onions will store whole for a short time, many onions that home gardeners grow don't store well for long—unless they slice and dry them.

While you may cry for a few hours and your house will smell like cooking onions for many hours as they dry, dried onions are extremely useful in the kitchen.

And they won't make you cry a second time when you use them.

White, yellow, or red onions can be dried. They should be harvested and allowed to sit in a warm, dry spot for a couple weeks before you prepare them for slicing and drying. Do not wash them until just before you peel them. *Yield: 2 cups*

DRIED ONIONS

What You Will Need

8-9 large onions (cooking types are best)

Mandoline or processor

Food dehydrator

Bag or containers for storage

Peel onions, remove roots, and then wash.

Slice onions ¼-inch thick or coarsely chop in processor. Slices should be cut into small pieces with a sharp knife.

Spread pieces in a single layer on dehydrator trays. Onions are best dried alone, as the flavor will soak into other foods dried with them.

Dry 3 to 9 hours, or until brittle. Cool and package.

Onion Powder and Salt

You can turn dried onions into onion powder or salt. Place the dried onions in a pepper grinder or food processor and grind to the fineness you prefer. Store in shaker bottles or containers with a little dry white rice to keep the powder from clumping. You can mix the powder with salt for onion salt. Dried parsley makes an attractive addition, as well.

PREPARING THE ONIONS

Peel the papery skins off onions and then wash them. Onions don't need pretreatment before drying.

Putting onions (well sealed) into the freezer for 20 minutes makes them easier to cut.

Onions can be sliced with a mandoline slicer, chopped in a food processor, or cut by hand. Small pieces dry faster.

Use a small fork to hold an onion steady as you slice it. To chop, stack slices and use a knife in a rocking motion.

Other Onion-Drying Methods

Onions can be dried in the oven at 140°F with the door cracked open an inch or two. It can take up to 18 hours.

Onions can be sun dried, too. Place on a tray in the sun when temperatures are hot and dry. It will take 2 to 3 days.

Don't dry other foods with onions or they will taste like onion!

SMOKED TURKEY JERKY

A TASTY TREAT FOR MEAT LOVERS ON THE TRAIL

Jerky is a perfect high-protein food to carry when hiking, hunting, or camping. It's also a good snack for busy office workers. This smoked turkey jerky is low fat and delicious. You must start with smoked turkey—not raw turkey. You can use either white or dark meat.

You can smoke a turkey you raised, or purchase smoked meat from a butcher. Wild turkey is a good candidate for this jerky. Many butcher shops offer smoking services for meat that you have raised or hunted.

The alcohol in the wine used for the marinade will evaporate off as the meat is precooked, but if you don't want to use wine, you can substitute white grape juice. *Yield: 20 ounces*

What You Will Need

5 pounds smoked turkey (do not use fresh turkey)

1 1/2 cups dry white wine

2/3 cup lemon juice

1/2 cup honey

1 tablespoon prepared yellow mustard

2 teaspoons liquid smoke (found with spices in grocery store)

2 teaspoons salt

1 teaspoon pepper

Cookie trays with wire racks

Containers for storage

SMOKED TURKEY JERKY

Partially freeze turkey. Slice ¼-inch thick. Cut slices 3 to 4 inches long and about 2 inches wide.

Put remaining ingredients in a large bowl; mix well. Dip strips in marinade, layer in a large pan, and pour remaining marinade over. Refrigerate overnight.

Pour everything into a large pot; boil 5 minutes. Drain strips and arrange on dehydrator racks so they are not touching.

Heat oven to 140°F and add trays; dry until jerky will crack but not snap when bent, 8 to 10 hours. Cool and package.

MAKE IT EASY

Don't have meat to make jerky with? Buy some deli meat. Choose lean meat that looks fresh and have it sliced ¼-inch thick. Poultry should be smoked for the best texture. Deli meat is usually precooked and won't need to be heat treated before making jerky. Buy the meat just before making jerky and keep it chilled until use. Each pound of meat makes about 4 ounces of jerky.

HOW TO CUT STRIPS

Partially frozen meat is easier to cut evenly. Make sure hands and equipment are clean before beginning.

Strips can be as long as your trays allow, but should only be ¼-inch thick and about 2 inches wide.

Cutting across the grain makes tender but brittle jerky; slicing with the grain of the meat makes chewy jerky.

While cutting meat, keep cut strips covered to prevent insect contamination.

HEAT TREATMENT

Strips should be kept in the refrigerator while they soak in the marinade. All the strips should be covered with marinade.

Boiling the strips in the marinade is the heat treatment to kill bacteria.

Begin timing when the marinade starts to boil, and boil the full 5 minutes.

Remove hot strips with tongs and allow the marinade to drain before placing them in the dryer. Do not reuse marinade.

BEEF JERKY

THIS IS MILDLY SPICY AND DELICIOUS

Drying is the oldest method of preserving food, and people have been drying meat for thousands of years. Wild game is very lean, and hunters generally consumed the tender fatty pieces immediately. Our domesticated beef is often very fatty, and fat increases the chance of spoilage. Choose the very leanest cuts of meat to make beef jerky, and cut off all visible fat.

Beef jerky can be seasoned in hundreds of ways. This recipe uses tomato juice to tenderize and flavor the meat and is very mild in flavor. If you like spicy jerky, add more red pepper or a dash of your favorite hot sauce or some horseradish.

Homemade jerky makes an excellent gift for those you love. *Yield: 20–32 ounces*

What You Will Need

5 pounds lean beef

2½ cups tomato juice

½ cup finely minced onion

½ cup firmly packed brown sugar

2 tablespoons Worcestershire sauce

1 teaspoon garlic powder

1½ teaspoons red pepper

1½ teaspoons salt

2 teaspoons liquid smoke (optional)

Food dehydrator

Containers for storage

BEEF JERKY

Slice ¼-inch thick, with the grain, into strips 2 inches wide and 3 to 4 inches long. Remove all fat.

Combine remaining ingredients. Dip strips in marinade, then layer in a pan. Pour remaining marinade on top. Refrigerate overnight.

Pour all ingredients into a pot and boil 5 minutes; drain. Lay strips on trays ¼ inch apart.

Follow dehydrator directions for drying meat. Dry about 8 hours; strips should crack but not snap when bent. Cool and pack for storage.

REMOVE ALL FAT

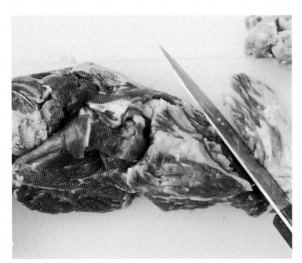

Meat that is still partially frozen is easier to trim and slice.

After slicing beef into strips, examine them for excess fat. The best-flavored jerky starts with lean meat.

Carefully trim off any fat. Fat increases the chance of spoilage and makes more mess while drying.

Meat will drip marinade and juices while it's drying. If too much fluid builds up in trays, empty and dry them, then return meat to dehydrator.

TESTING FOR DRYNESS

In a dehydrator, meat can take 10 hours to dry, but it may be done in as little as 3 hours.

After 3 hours, check the jerky every hour. Remove a piece and bend it. If it cracks at the bend but doesn't snap in two, it is done.

Let jerky cool before wrapping it. Store jerky in a tightly closed container or vacuum seal.

Homemade jerky should only be stored 1 month at room temperature. Freezing or refrigerating prolongs storage.

VENISON JERKY

TURN VENISON INTO A CHEWY, FLAVORFUL TREAT

If you are a hunter, you often have odds and ends of venison (deer meat) that could make good jerky. Venison is lean meat and easily turns into flavorful jerky. Properly frozen venison can be thawed and turned into jerky just before your next hunting trip.

Make sure you field dress and chill your deer as soon as possible after the kill. Spoiled or old meat will not be made safe by drying. Meat contaminated by spilled fecal or gut contents should not be used.

Venison often has a "gamey" taste. This marinade recipe replaces that taste with a delicious, mildly spicy flavor. Unsweetened pineapple juice can replace the lemon, and if you like it hotter, add some red pepper. *Yield: About 2 pounds*

What You Will Need

5 pounds venison

3/4 cup soy sauce

1/2 cup honey

1/2 cup lemon juice

2 tablespoons Worcestershire sauce

1 teaspoon onion powder

1 teaspoon garlic powder

1/2 teaspoon black pepper

1/2 teaspoon salt

Food dehydrator

Containers for storage

VENISON JERKY

Partially freeze meat. Slice with the grain, ¼-inch thick. Cut into strips 2 inches wide by 3 to 4 inches long.

Combine remaining ingredients. Dip strips to coat. Layer in pan. Pour remaining marinade over meat. Refrigerate overnight.

Pour all ingredients into a pot. Boil 10 minutes; drain. Arrange on dehydrator trays so strips are not touching.

Follow dehydrator instructions for drying meat. Dry until strips crack but don't snap when bent, about 8 hours. Cool and package.

Pemmican

This high-energy food, used by native peoples for thousands of years, is made of fats and dried meat. Place jerky in a food processor and pulverize to powder. For every cup of meat, melt 1 cup rendered beef fat or unhydrogenated lard. Mix melted fat with meat; form into bars. You can add ⅓ cup dried, pulverized fruit to each batch. Don't add salt!

Important

Jerky made at home without artificial preservatives will be good for only about a month at room temperature. If you refrigerate it, jerky storage time increases to 2 to 3 months. Freezing jerky keeps it safe for up to 12 months. Vacuum packages are great; otherwise tightly wrap jerky in plastic wrap and put that in an airtight container. If you use plastic storage bags, expel as much air as possible.

MARINATE OVERNIGHT

The marinade tenderizes and flavors the meat. Make sure all the meat is covered by the marinade.

Meat must be refrigerated while marinating. Leave the strips in the marinade for 8 to 12 hours.

The marinade is used to cook the meat for pretreatment. After boiling for 10 minutes, drain the meat and discard the marinade; never reuse it.

Arrange meat on trays so pieces don't touch or touch the walls.

FOLLOW DEHYDRATOR INSTRUCTIONS

Read the instructions that come with your food dehydrator for drying meat.

Some companies do not recommend preheating or instruct you to heat meat after drying.

The USDA recommends you always precook meat for food safety, regardless of the manufacturer's instructions. If you do this, meat doesn't need heat treatment after drying.

Be sure to follow all other instructions for arranging or rotating trays and for the settings to use.

NO-SALT DILL PICKLES

IF YOU ARE ON A SALT-RESTRICTED DIET BUT CRAVE PICKLES, TRY THESE

Yes, you can have pickles if you are on a low-sodium diet. Most pickles are loaded with sodium, and commercial pickles may have more salt than homemade pickles. This recipe gives you some very tasty dill pickles without salt.

This recipe uses horseradish, which is very "hot" spicy. You can leave it out if you don't like the flavor.

This recipe makes a lot of pickles. You may want to cut it in half the first time you make it to see if you want to change the spices to suit your taste. The flavors will intensify a bit as the pickles sit, so wait for a month to make your decision. *Yield: 8 quarts*

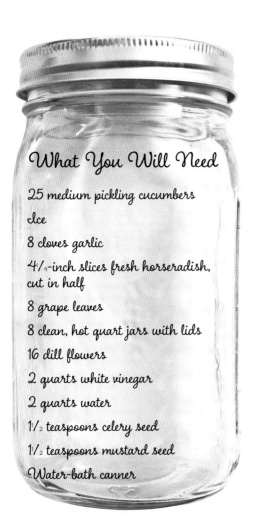

What You Will Need

25 medium pickling cucumbers

Ice

8 cloves garlic

4¼-inch slices fresh horseradish, cut in half

8 grape leaves

8 clean, hot quart jars with lids

16 dill flowers

2 quarts white vinegar

2 quarts water

1½ teaspoons celery seed

1½ teaspoons mustard seed

Water-bath canner

NO-SALT DILL PICKLES

Scrub cucumbers, and place in ice water for 12 hours in refrigerator.

Drain cucumbers, slice off blossom end, and cut into spears, about ½-inch thick.

Put 1 garlic clove, ½ slice horseradish, and 1 grape leaf in each jar. Pack with spears to half full, position dill flower on each side of jar, and continue filling to ½ inch from rim.

Bring vinegar, water, celery seed, and mustard seed to boiling. Pour over cucumbers to ½ inch from top. Remove bubbles, wipe rims, top with lids, and process.

Water-Bath Canner Processing Times for Quarts				
Altitude in Feet	0-1,000	1,001-3,000	3,001-6,000	6,001+
Processing Time	15 minutes	20 minutes	25 minutes	25 minutes

Grape Leaves

Grape leaves are a natural way to make pickles crisper. Some ethnic markets sell grape leaves, or you can pick the leaves of any cultivated or wild grape. Just make sure the leaves haven't been sprayed with pesticides. To store leaves, wash and dry them, then layer them with salt in a nonmetallic container. Rinse before use, and they won't add any salt to the pickles.

ADDING THE SEASONINGS

The grape leaves make the pickles crisper. They should be fresh or preserved whole in salt.

Peel the horseradish like a carrot. Slice it in very thin rounds, almost see-through. Then cut rounds in half.

Lay a grape leaf on the bottom of each jar. Then add the garlic and horseradish.

Position the dill flowers about halfway up the jars, yellow side out, as a decorative touch to the jars. They also add flavor.

ADDING THE LIQUID

After the jars are packed with cucumbers and spices, they are ready for the pickling fluid.

Bring the vinegar mixture just to a boil, then immediately ladle or pour it into the jars.

Don't let the vinegar boil too long or the acidity will be lessened, which affects food safety.

After the pickles are processed, let them sit for a few weeks before tasting to intensify the flavors.

BREAD & BUTTER PICKLES

THESE PICKLES USE A SUGAR SUBSTITUTE FOR SWEET, BUT BETTER-FOR-YOU, PICKLES

Bread-and-butter pickles have a unique sweet-and-sour taste. The sweetness in this recipe comes from an artificial sweetener. They are a great treat for people with diabetes craving sweet pickles.

Certain spices are part of the bread-and-butter flavor. You can modify the spices if you like, but if you do, they may not taste like the pickles you remember.

This recipe uses some salt, but the pickles are not as salty as some pickle recipes, and the salt can be totally eliminated if you like.

Serve bread-and-butter pickles between slices of buttered bread like the old-timers do or on a relish plate. They are delicious either way. *Yield: 5 pints*

What You Will Need

4 pounds small pickling cucumbers
2 medium peeled and sliced onions
1 garlic clove
1 tablespoon canning salt
Ice
4 cups cider vinegar
1 cup water
1 tablespoon mustard seed
1 tablespoon celery seed
1½ teaspoons turmeric
½ teaspoon ground cinnamon
½ teaspoon ground allspice
½ teaspoon ground cloves
3 cups Splenda
5 clean, hot pint jars and lids
Water-bath canner

BREAD-AND-BUTTER PICKLES

Scrub cucumbers; slice off blossom end and discard. Do not peel. Slice cucumbers into ¼-inch rounds. Add sliced onions to cucumbers.

Crush garlic clove, add with salt to cucumbers and onions, and toss to mix. Cover mixture with ice; refrigerate 3 hours.

Bring vinegar, water, and spices to a boil and simmer 5 minutes. Add Splenda and stir to dissolve.

Drain cucumbers and onions; discard garlic. Pack into hot jars. Add hot liquid to ½ inch from top. Remove bubbles, wipe rims, add lids, and process.

Water-Bath Canner Processing Times for Pints				
Altitude in Feet	0-1,000	1,001-3,000	3,001-6,000	6,001+
Processing Time	15 minutes	15 minutes	15 minutes	20 minutes

Important

Not all artificial sweeteners are equal when it comes to canning. Some sweeteners have a bitter taste after heating. Sucralose is recommended for pickle recipes. Another choice may be one of the new stevia-based sweeteners (such as rebiana), which Japan is using in commercial pickles. When you use an artificial sweetener, don't assume you should use the same amount as sugar. Follow the label for figuring out equivalent measures.

PREPARING THE VEGETABLES

Traditionally bread-and-butter pickles are cut in wavy slices, but you can cut yours any way you like. The onions are just thinly sliced.

Don't make the cucumber slices too thick. Thin slices will be crisper; ¼ inch is about right.

The salting and ice are to make the pickles crisper. Using crushed ice works best. Keep pickles in the refrigerator during the crisping.

After draining the pickles, immediately pack the jars to ½ inch from rim.

ADDING THE SWEETENER

Do not boil this pickling liquid; it should just simmer for the 5 minutes.

Add the sweetener at the end of the simmering period. Turn off the heat and stir it in until it's dissolved.

Pour the liquid while it's still hot over the packed jars. Make sure all the slices are covered.

After running a bubble stick through the jars, you may need to adjust the fluid levels before processing.

LOW-SUGAR PEACH JAM

NEVER FEEL GUILTY WHEN YOU ENJOY THIS TREAT

This wonderful sunny and sweet jam won't leave you feeling deprived if you need to lower your sugar intake. You can enjoy its flavor on your morning toast or muffin without worry. One tablespoon of this jam contains roughly 10 calories.

You can never totally remove the sugar from a jam or jelly because fruit has natural sugar. However, you reduce the sugar content and the calories by adding pectin to replace the thickening qualities of sugar and artificial sweeteners to make it taste sweeter. If you don't mind your jam a little less sweet, you could leave out the artificial sweetener entirely. A sweet fruit like peaches still makes a tasty jam without sweetening. *Yield: 3 half-pint containers*

What You Will Need

4 cups peeled, chopped peaches

Food processor

1 tablespoon lemon juice

½ teaspoon ascorbic acid crystals

1 1.75-ounce package powdered regular pectin

3½ teaspoons liquid artificial sweetener of your choice

3 sterilized, freezer-safe half-pint jars and lids

LOW-SUGAR PEACH JAM

Put peaches in boiling water and then in cold water; slip off the skins. Remove pits and chop. Puree in processor.

Put peach puree in a saucepan with lemon juice, ascorbic acid, and pectin. Bring to a boil and boil 1 minute, stirring constantly.

Remove from heat. Stir in sweetener; continue stirring 2 minutes.

Pour into jars, cool, and top with lids. Freeze any jars that will not be used in 1 week. Keep opened jars refrigerated.

COOKING THE PUREE

The pectin needs the ascorbic acid and lemon juice to help thicken the product; don't omit these.

Don't add the sweetener to the mix until the heat is turned off. Too much heat will make it bitter.

Any artificial liquid sweeteners will work fine. Don't substitute powdered sweeteners in this recipe.

Keep stirring the mixture for at least 2 minutes after you add the sweetener to blend it well and help the mixture thicken.

THIS JAM MUST BE FROZEN

Make sure your jars are sterilized and kept submerged in hot water before filling.

The jars probably won't seal as they sit and cool, but that is okay since the jam will be frozen. Lids should fit tightly.

Make sure the containers are cool and the jam has thickened and set before you place the jars in the freezer.

This jam must be frozen for storage. It will mold or spoil if kept at room temperature.

REDUCED-SUGAR GRAPE JELLY

THIS RECIPE CUTS THE SUGAR AND THE CALORIES, BUT NOT THE TASTE

If you love peanut butter and jelly sandwiches but worry about all those calories from regular jelly, or have to restrict your sugar intake, this recipe can help you. This jelly isn't totally sugar free, because all fruit has natural sugars, but it is reduced in calories without sacrificing flavor and texture. Each table-spoon of this jelly has roughly 11 calories.

This is a different method of thickening fruit juice from the Low-Sugar Peach Jam recipe. This gelatin method works well with grapes, which have a small amount of natural pectin to aid thickening. Apple juice would work equally well with this recipe. You can use home-canned or commercially prepared unsweet-ened juice for this recipe. *Yield: 3 half-pint containers*

What You Will Need

2 packages (2 tablespoons) unflavored gelatin

2 tablespoons lemon juice

3 cups unsweetened pure grape juice

2 tablespoons artificial liquid sweetener of choice (optional)

3 sterilized, hot half-pint jars and lids

REDUCED-SUGAR GRAPE JELLY

Mix the gelatin with the lemon juice and stir into a soft paste.

Place the grape juice in a saucepan. Heat ,and just before boiling add the gelatin. Bring to a rolling boil, stirring constantly.

Boil 1 minute, then remove from heat. Add sweetener, if desired. Stir an additional 1 minute.

Pour the jelly into jars and top with lids. Store jelly in the refrigerator or freeze for long-term storage.

Gelatin

The gelatin used in this recipe is not the packaged gelatin you make desserts from. It is unflavored and may be found with either flavored gelatins or in the canning-supplies section. All gelatin is made from animal products. Jelly made from gelatin may not be considered kosher or halal foods and may violate religious customs or offend vegetarians. Kosher gelatin is available in some areas.

Easy Meatballs

These meatballs are tasty and reduced in calories. Defrost frozen meatballs, or make and brown about 3 pounds. Combine 12 ounces chili sauce, 16 ounces grape jelly, and 1 teaspoon oregano in a saucepan over medium heat; stir until mixture is bubbly and jelly melted. Pour over meatballs and simmer for 30 minutes with the lid on. *Yield: 3 pounds*

SOFTENING THE GELATIN

First place the powdered gelatin in a small bowl and add the lemon juice. Stir until they make a soft paste.

Heat the grape juice to just before boiling and stir in the gelatin paste.

Bring the mixture to a full, vigorous boil and start timing. Boil 1 minute, stirring the mixture quickly and constantly.

Turn off the heat and add the artificial sweetener, if using, stirring all the while. Stir for at least 1 more minute.

FILLING THE JARS

The jars should be sterilized and kept under hot water until ready to use.

Pour the jelly while still hot into the jars. It will look a bit thin. Top with the lids.

Let the jars sit to cool and gel. They may not seal, but that's okay.

After the jelly feels cool and looks set (thick), place in the freezer for long-term storage. Refrigerate opened jars; this jelly will spoil if left at room temperature.

LOW-SUGAR VERY BERRY JAM

A MELODY OF TANGY SWEET BERRIES IN A MOUTH-PLEASING, DELICIOUS JAM

You'll be proud to serve this simple recipe at any brunch or tea or even to give it as a gift.

You can use any granular sugar substitute in this recipe, but sucralose is probably the best one for the job. If you enjoy the tart flavor of fresh fruit, leave the sweetener out altogether.

If you don't have all the berries available fresh, you can use frozen berries that have been thawed and drained.

Remember that fruit has sugar, and this jam won't be sugar free, just lower in sugar and calories. *Yield: 5 half-pint containers*

What You Will Need

1 cup raspberries

1 cup blackberries

2 cups cleaned, hulled, sliced strawberries

1 package no-sugar pectin

1½ cup granular sugar substitute

5 sterilized half-pint jars and lids

LOW-SUGAR VERY BERRY JAM

Wash the raspberries and blackberries. Combine all the berries in a large bowl.

In a separate bowl, mix the no-sugar pectin into the granular sugar substitute.

Crush the berries with a spoon. Then slowly add the pectin–sugar substitute mix, blending well. Stir until sugar substitute is dissolved and mix thickens—about 3 minutes.

Pour jam into jars. Let sit 5 minutes, then stir to redistribute fruit pieces. Add lids and refrigerate. Freeze jam that won't be used within a week.

BRINGING OUT THE JUICE

Blend together the granular sugar substitute and the no-sugar pectin.

Put the berries in a large bowl and crush them with a spoon or potato masher. You can also use a blender, but leave the berries a bit chunky.

When you have juice, slowly add the pectin mixture, stirring or pulse blending as you go.

Keep stirring; the mixture should thicken in about 3 minutes. If the mixture doesn't seem to be thick enough, add another teaspoon pectin.

BLENDING FRUIT IN JARS

Jars for this recipe should be sterilized before using and be freezer safe.

After all the pectin is dissolved, fill the jars and let them gel about 5 minutes. As the jam thickens, fruit pieces float to the top.

To make the jars more attractive, use a spatula to stir the fruit pieces back through the jam after it has jelled.

Put lids on the jars and store any that won't be used in a week in the freezer.

SNAPPY PICKLED ONIONS

HOT, SPICY, AND SALT FREE, THESE ONIONS PLEASE THE PALATE

You won't miss the salt in these ooh-la-la spicy pickled onions. It's the horseradish with the red pepper that gives them their fiery zing and brings tears of joy to the eyes. Bring these out at your Super Bowl party or your neighborhood barbecue. Use them as a garnish on a steak platter or liven up a bland relish tray.

Use small garden onions or special pickling onions for this recipe. Small white onion sets that are sold for spring planting also work in this recipe.

Don't reduce the sugar or vinegar in this recipe, but you can reduce the horseradish and pepper if you don't like the heat. These get hotter as they sit in storage. *Yield: 4 pints*

What You Will Need

8 cups tiny white onions

Water

1 cup white sugar

3½ cups white vinegar

4 bay leaves

4 ¼-inch-thick slices fresh horseradish root

4 teaspoons red pepper

4 clean, hot pint jars and lids

Water-bath canner

SNAPPY PICKLED ONIONS

Dip onions in boiling water. Slip off skins and remove roots.

Bring sugar and vinegar to a boil in a large saucepan. Add onions, boil 1 minute.

Place 1 bay leaf, 1 slice horseradish, and 1 teaspoon red pepper in each jar. Fill jars with onions.

Pour cooking fluid into jars to fill to ½ inch from rim. Remove bubbles, wipe rims, top with lids, and process.

Water-Bath Canner Processing Times for Pints				
Altitude in Feet	0-1,000	1,001-3,000	3,001-6,000	6,001+
Processing Time	10 minutes	15 minutes	15 minutes	20 minutes

Recipe Variation

Cauliflower Snappers: Cauliflower also makes an excellent "snapper" and may be easier to find late in the summer. Soak cauliflower heads in salt water for 30 minutes; drain. Break the cauliflower into small florets, removing any woody parts. Then follow the recipe for onions, except boil the cauliflower florets for 3 minutes. Onions and cauliflower "clash" and shouldn't be mixed.

PREPARING HORSERADISH

To make the horseradish slices, scrub horseradish root thoroughly. You can peel it like a carrot or slice without peeling.

Use a sharp knife to cut the firm horseradish into thin, almost see-through, slices. Just be sure they are no more than ¼-inch thick.

If the horseradish root is large in diameter, you may want to cut slices in half.

If you can't find fresh horseradish, you might find jarred minced or sliced horseradish in the store.

ADDING THE "HEAT"

The spices and horseradish are added to each jar equally before the onions. The onions will get hotter as they sit in storage.

Lift the onions from the vinegar with a slotted spoon and fill the jars. Pack firmly, but don't smash onions.

When the jars are filled, pour hot cooking fluid over them to ½ inch from rim.

Make sure to use a bubble stick and adjust the fluid after bubbles are released.

WHAT WENT WRONG

A QUICK CHART TO HELP YOU DECIDE WHAT TO DO DIFFERENTLY
NEXT TIME

Problem	What Went Wrong	What to Remember Next Time
Lids didn't seal	Jar cracked, rim chipped, food on rim, handling jars while hot—**Do not taste or use.**	Check jars and rims carefully. Don't disturb jars while cooling.
Jars lost fluid during processing	Air bubbles rose, pressure fluctuated too much, food boiled over, jars not covered in water canner—**Do not open jars after processing to add more fluid.**	Remove bubbles before processing. Leave the recommended space to jar rim. Keep pressure from fluctuating. Keep jars covered with water.
Cloudy or discolored fluid in jars or sediment	Minerals in water, additives in salt or spices, starch or pigments in food, possible spoilage—**Check with an expert.**	Use soft water. Use canning salt. Some natural pigments and starches are harmless; sediment from spices is harmless.
Spoiled food	Improper processing type or time, jars didn't seal, improper storage—**Do not taste food—check with an expert.**	Follow directions for type of processing. Time processing correctly. Make sure jars seal before storing.
Pickle problems	See sidebar in Chapter 3, page 32	
Jelly doesn't set	Over- or undercooking, not enough acid or sugar, using the wrong pectin, too much water, batch was too large	Follow the recipe. Don't double batches. Use the proper pectin.
Mold on jelly	Improper processing, lids didn't seal, not refrigerated/ frozen if needed—**Discard the jam or jelly.**	Follow processing directions, make sure lids seal, freeze or refrigerate freezer jams promptly.
Freezer burn	Air getting into loose or torn packages or sealed inside, in freezer too long	Remove as much air as possible from packages. Use freezer products not storage. Rewrap damaged food promptly. Rotate and use food before it's too old.
Off flavors and colors in frozen food	Fat going rancid, not blanching or pre-cooking foods, picking up other foods odors	Use fresh meat. Precook or blanch according to recipe. Don't store too long. Tightly seal packages.
Dry food molding	Not enough drying time, improper storage, packaging while hot—**Don't use molded food.**	Thoroughly dry foods. Cool before packaging. Store in airtight containers.
Insects or larvae in dried food	Food dried outside, food not stored properly—**Don't use food.**	Cover food drying outside and pasteurize before storage. Store in tightly sealed containers.

WHERE TO GET HELP

FINDING YOUR ALTITUDE

Go to www.weather.gov. You will see a United States map; click on your area, which will bring up a map of the region around you. Click on the map closest to where you live. Look for the altitude that appears under the "Point Forecast" that comes up on the page. This works for most areas of the United States.

You can also call your county Cooperative Extension office or local USDA conservation district office and they can give you your general altitude. Look under "government" in the phone book or find the number online.

GETTING PRESSURE GAUGES CHECKED FOR ACCURACY

Call your county Cooperative Extension office first. The office is an outreach office of a university or college and many have educators who specialize in food and nutrition. They can test your dial at the office or tell you where to get it checked. Find your Cooperative Extension office at www.csrees.usda .gov. Click on your state and then your county. Or look in the phone book under "government."

The manufacturer of your canner can also check the gauges or suggest a place to have them checked. There should be a number in your instruction booklet. If the instructions are missing, you can look up the contact information online.

National Presto Industries also offers pressure gauge checking. They can be reached at 3925 N. Hastings Way, Eau Claire, WI 54703; (800) 877-0441; www.gopresto.com.

You can purchase new gauges to replace those that are defective.

HOTLINES

Ball and Kerr: (800) 240-3340

Kraft Foods: (800) 431-1001

Pomona and Mrs. Wages: (413) 772-6816

USDA Meat and Poultry: (800) 535-4555

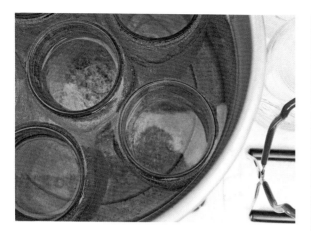

BOOKS & WEBSITES

BOOKS

When purchasing books, look for the most up-to-date editions. New food safety research has determined that some older canning recipes are not safe. Books published before 1980 may have serious safety flaws, and research is changing what we know about food preservation every year.

Ball Blue Book 100th Anniversary Edition
Available at www.freshpreserving.com and at many bookstores, including Amazon.

New USDA Complete Guide to Home Canning
Available at www.extension.purdue.edu/store

So Easy To Preserve
Published by University of Georgia, available at www.soeasytopreserve.com

WEBSITES

National Center for Home Food Preservation
www.uga.edu/nchfp/index.html
Most current research-based information based at the University of Georgia; lots of helpful online information.

Pick Your Own
www.pickyourown.org
Directions for canning all kinds of fresh produce. They also have supplies for sale.

Simply Canning
www.simplycanning.com
Good canning information.

Using and Caring for a Pressure Canner
www.Cals.uidaho.edu/edComm/pdf/PNW/PNW 0421.pdf
Learn more about pressure canners.

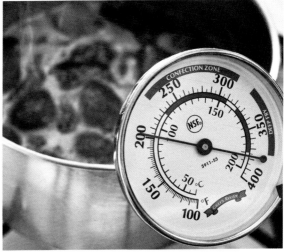

MORE RECIPE VARIATIONS

SUNNY BLEND
(Variation of the Mixed Fruit in Syrup on pages 48–49)
Use apricots, pineapple, papaya, and orange slices. Follow recipe as directed.

PEACH PIE FILLING
(Variation of the Apple Pie Filling on pages 52–53)
Use 6 quarts peeled, pitted, and sliced peaches. Place peach slices in color preservative solution and blanch as in recipe. Use 7 cups sugar, 2 cups plus 2 tablespoons Clear Jel, 5¼ cups water, and 1¾ cups lemon juice; add 1 teaspoon cinnamon. Follow recipe as written.

PLUM SAUCE
(Variation of the Peach Dipping Sauce on pages 62–63)
Use 4 cups peeled, pitted, and chopped plums instead of peaches.

RASPBERRY JAM
(Variation of the Strawberry Jam on pages 64–65)
Use 9 cups cleaned, crushed raspberries in place of the strawberries.

BLACKBERRY JELLY
(Variation of the Grape Jelly on pages 66–67)
Use 10 cups clean blackberries, 3 cups sugar, and ¾ cup water. Crush the blackberries and add the water. Bring to a boil, reduce heat, and simmer 5 minutes. Pour into jelly bag and proceed as for Grape Jelly.

APRICOT PRESERVES
(Variation of the Peach Preserves on pages 70–71)
Use 8 cups peeled, pitted apricots in place of the peaches.

PLUM PRESERVES
(Variation of the Peach Preserves on pages 70–71)
Use 8 cups peeled, pitted plums in place of peaches.

SOURCES FOR EQUIPMENT, SUPPLIES & INGREDIENTS

CANNING SUPPLIES

All American Canner.com
www.allamericancanner.com

Ball
A source for jars and lids.
www.freshpreserving.com

Canning Pantry
www.canningpantry.com

Canning Supply
www.canningsupply.com

Freundcontainers.com
Unusual canning jars, decorative jelly jars, and so on.
www.freundcontainers.com

EQUIPMENT

Lehmans
Good source for all types of home-preserving supplies. They have lots of unique items.
www.lehmans.com

Pressure Cooker Outlet
www.pressurecooker-outlet.com

INGREDIENTS

Clear Jel, Pectin, Kosher Gelatin

Amazon Grocery Delivery
www.agrocerydelivery.com

Kitchen Krafts
www.kitchenkrafts.com

Kosher Gelatin
www.koshergelatin.com

Pomona Pectin
www.pomonapectin.com

Groceries

Amazon Grocery Delivery
Hard-to-find local items may turn up here.
www.agrocerydelivery.com

Local Harvest
www.localharvest.org

National Directory of Farmers' Markets and Fruit Stands
www.fruitstands.com

USDA
Farmers' markets near you are listed with the USDA.
apps.ams.usda.gov/FarmersMarkets

Spices

Mrs. Wages
store.mrswagesstore.com

Penzey's Spices
www.penzeys.com

wholespice.com
www.wholespice.com

WEIGHTS & MEASURES

MEASUREMENTS

3 teaspoons = 1 tablespoon
2 tablespoons = 1 fluid ounce
4 tablespoons = ¼ cup
1 cup = 8 fluid ounces
2 cups = 1 pint
2 pints = 1 quart
4 quarts = 1 gallon
8 quarts produce = 1 peck
4 pecks produce = 1 bushel

The weight of dry measures varies by product.
1 pound canning salt = about 1⅓ cups
1 pound white sugar = about 2 cups
1 pound firmly packed brown sugar = 2⅔ cups

METRIC EQUIVALENTS

59.15 milliliters = 4 tablespoons
250 milliliters = 1.05 cups
1 liter = 1.06 quarts
1 ounce = 28 grams
1 pound = 454 grams

TEMPERATURE

To convert temperature from Fahrenheit to Celsius, subtract 32 from the Fahrenheit temperature, then multiply by 5, then divide by 9.

APPROXIMATE YIELDS OF PRODUCE

(Yields are for canned or frozen—not dried.) Yields vary with the size of produce, amount of waste, and other factors.

Apples: 1 pound is 6 medium and yields about 3 cups chopped. 1 bushel will fill about 18 quart jars.

Apricots: 1 pound is about 8 to 10 apricots and yields about 2 cups chopped.

Beans (green): 1 pound yields about 3 cups cut; 1 bushel will fill about 18 quarts.

Beets: 1 pound beets is 4 to 6 medium and yields 3½ cups diced.

Blueberries: 1 pound yields about 3 cups.

Cabbage: 1 pound cabbage yields about 3½ cups sliced; 50 pounds fills about 20 quarts.

Carrots: 1 pound is about 4 large carrots and yields 2½ cups diced; 2 pounds are needed for each quart.

Cherries: 2½ pounds yield 4 cups whole and pitted.

Corn: 16 to 20 ears yield about 2 quarts kernels cut from the cob.

Cranberries: 1 pound yields 4 cups whole.

Cucumbers: 1 pound is about 2 large and yields 2½ cups sliced; 6 pounds yield about 1 gallon slices.

Grapes: 1 pound yields about 4 cups whole.

Onions: 1 pound is 3 large and yields about 2½ cups chopped.

Peaches: 1 pound is 3 to 5 peaches and yields about 2½ cups chopped or sliced.

Peas: 1 pound peas in the pod yields about 1 cup shelled peas.

Pears: 1 pound is 4 to 5 pears and yields 2½ cups chopped.

Peppers (hot): Depending on type, 1 pound raw yields about 1 cup cored and chopped.

Peppers (sweet-bell types): 1 pound is 4 large and yields about 2 cups chopped.

Plums: 1 pound is 12 to 20 plums and yields 2 cups sliced.

Potatoes (sweet): 3 pounds yield about 4 cups chopped.

Potatoes (white): 3 pounds yield about 4 cups sliced; 1 bushel fills about 20 quarts.

Pumpkin: 1 pound yields 2 cups chunks.

Raspberries, Blackberries: Each quart box weighs about 1½ pounds and yields about 3 cups whole berries.

Strawberries: A dry quart box yields 3 cups halved berries.

Tomatoes: 1 pound is 4 medium tomatoes and yields 3 cups sliced; 1 bushel slicing tomatoes yields about 18 quarts.

Zucchini: 1 pound yields about 2 cups diced.

METRIC CONVERSION TABLES

APPROXIMATE U.S. METRIC EQUIVALENTS

Liquid Ingredients

U.S. MEASURES	METRIC	U.S. MEASURES	METRIC
¼ TSP.	1.23 ML	2 TBSP.	29.57 ML
½ TSP.	2.36 ML	3 TBSP.	44.36 ML
¾ TSP.	3.70 ML	¼ CUP	59.15 ML
1 TSP.	4.93 ML	½ CUP	118.30 ML
1¼ TSP.	6.16 ML	1 CUP	236.59 ML
1½ TSP.	7.39 ML	2 CUPS OR 1 PT.	473.18 ML
1¾ TSP.	8.63 ML	3 CUPS	709.77 ML
2 TSP.	9.86 ML	4 CUPS OR 1 QT.	946.36 ML
1 TBSP.	14.79 ML	4 QTS. OR 1 GAL.	3.79 L

Dry Ingredients

U.S. MEASURES	METRIC	U.S. MEASURES		METRIC
1/16 OZ.	2 (1.8) G	2⅘ OZ.		80 G
⅛ OZ.	3½ (3.5) G	3 OZ.		85 (84.9) G
¼ OZ.	7 (7.1) G	3½ OZ.		100 G
½ OZ.	15 (14.2) G	4 OZ.		115 (113.2) G
¾ OZ.	21 (21.3) G	4½ OZ.		125 G
⅞ OZ.	25 G	5¼ OZ.		150 G
1 OZ.	30 (28.3) G	8⅞ OZ.		250 G
1¾ OZ.	50 G	16 OZ.	1 LB.	454 G
2 OZ.	60 (56.6) G	17⅗ OZ.	1 LIVRE	500 G

GLOSSARY

Altitude: Height above sea level.

Ascorbic acid: Vitamin C—it's used as a preservative for color in canned fruits and to acidify some fruits. It comes in a variety of forms. Follow directions on the package when mixing color preservative solutions or substituting another form for crystalline ascorbic acid.

Blanching: The process of quickly heating food in boiling water then quickly cooling it. It stops enzyme activity that changes color, texture, and taste in preserved foods.

Brine, Brining: A salty solution used to preserve food, particularly pickles. Brining means adding the salt solution or letting food soak in it.

Bubble stick: Any small, flat nonmetallic object that is run around the inside of a filled jar to release tiny bubbles that cling to the jar sides and food.

Citric acid: A natural product derived from citrus fruit that is added to foods to acidify them or to preserve color.

Dehydrator: A machine that heats food at a low temperature so that it dries instead of cooks.

Enzymes: Proteins in foods that control complex biochemical processes; they can be inactivated by heat, such as by blanching.

Fermentation: The breakdown of carbohydrates by microorganisms, producing lactic acid as a by-product, which can preserve food and changes its color and taste.

Lid: In canning this refers to a small flat piece of metal with a band of adhesive. It fits over the mouth of a jar and when heated and then cooled, it seals to the jar rim and creates a vacuum inside the jar.

Mandoline: A kitchen utensil that slices food when it is slid over a series of blades. It's generally operated by hand.

Pressure canner: Food in jars is put inside this large pot with a small amount of water. The lid seals out air and when heated, steam creates pressure, which cooks food at a higher temperature than boiling water does and kills the microorganisms in low-acid foods.

Processing: In canning this refers to the heating treatment that makes food safe to eat when stored at room temperature.

Produce: Vegetables and fruits in general.

Rim: The top edge of a canning jar.

Screw band: A grooved metal ring that has an open area in the center. It screws onto the grooves in a jar top and holds the lid down during processing.

Water-bath canner: A large pot that allows jars of food to be totally submerged in water. The water is brought to boiling to heat treat acidic foods and kill microorganisms that cause food spoilage.

INDEX

venison
 Canned Venison, 150–51
 Venison Jerky, 218–19

W
Weiner Relish, Old-Fashioned,
 146–47
White Cherry Fudge, 205

Z
Zucchini Bread, 175
Zucchini, Grated, 174–75